To: ______________________________

The earth is filled with your love,
O LORD; teach me your decrees.

PSALM 119:64

From: ______________________________

God's Words of Life for Leaders

ISBN 0-310-97901-3

Excerpts taken from: *The Leadership Bible: Leadership Principles from God's Word; New International Version.*

Requests for information should be addressed to:
Inspirio, The gift group of Zondervan
Grand Rapids, Michigan 49530

Senior Editor: Gwen Ellis
Project Editor: Sarah Hupp
Designer: Big Picture Design

Printed in China

01 02 03/HK/7 6 5 4 3

God's Words of Life for Leaders

from the
New International Version

MEERBUSEN VON MEXICO
Black Hills
Platte
Canadian

Table of Contents

God's Words of Life for Leaders on

God's Words of Life on

Accountability

Standards of Accountability

Effective leaders hold themselves accountable just like everyone else on the team. Maintaining such accountability involves seeking complete honesty. Skilled leaders consistently receive feedback from those who work above them, beside them and for them. A failure to provide a structure for such accountability will lead to a crisis of character and leadership.

David was the king who had it all. He enjoyed an intimate walk with God, a family, a stable political position and an unbroken string of military victories. The one thing he didn't have was Uriah's wife. And that was what he wanted. While the rest of his army was at war, he stayed at home. Apparently, nobody dared question the wisdom of his hiatus. With nobody to answer to, David committed the acts of adultery and murder described in 2 Samuel 11.

This tragedy underscores what can happen when leaders fail to create a structure in which they are answerable for how they spend

Accountability

their private and professional time. While David could hide his sins from his associates, he couldn't hide them from God. One day the prophet Nathan confronted David. The king discovered that even kings are accountable for their actions.

Wise leaders don't wait for a crisis to establish accountability. They establish structures and relationships that harness their sin and unleash their potential. Ultimately, God will hold every leader accountable. Do you have someone to whom you are accountable for your private and professional life?

Be shepherds of God's flock that is under your care, serving as overseers —not because you must, but because you are willing, as God wants you to be; not greedy for money, but eager to serve; not lording it over those entrusted to you, but being examples to the flock. And when the Chief Shepherd appears, you will receive the crown of glory that will never fade away.

1 Peter 5:2 –4

God's Words of Life on

Accountability

You, O God, do see trouble and grief; you consider it to take it in hand. The victim commits himself to you; you are the helper of the fatherless.

PSALM 10:14

The eyes of the LORD range throughout the earth to strengthen those whose hearts are fully committed to him.

2 CHRONICLES 16:9

Blessed is the man who does not walk in the counsel of the wicked or stand in the way of sinners or sit in the seat of mockers.

PSALM 1:1

Moses' father-in-law replied, ". . . . You and these people who come to you will only wear yourselves out. The work is too heavy for you; you cannot handle it alone. Listen now to me and I will give you some advice, and may God be with you. You must be the people's representative before God and bring their disputes to him. Teach them the decrees and laws, and show them the way to live and the duties they are to perform. But select capable men from all the people —men who fear God, trustworthy men who hate dishonest gain — and appoint them as officials over thousands, hundreds, fifties and tens. Have them serve as judges for the people at all times, but have them bring every difficult case to you; the simple cases they can decide themselves. That will make your load lighter, because they will share it with you. If you do this and God so commands, you will be able to stand the strain, and all these people will go home satisfied."

Exodus 18:17 –23

Since an overseer is entrusted with God's work, he must be blameless —not overbearing, not quick-tempered, not given to drunkenness, not violent, not pursuing dishonest gain. Rather he must be hospitable, one who loves what is good, who is self-controlled, upright, holy and disciplined. He must hold firmly to the trustworthy message as it has been taught, so that he can encourage others by sound doctrine and refute those who oppose it.

Titus 1:7 –9

Change

The Innovation of Change

"Why do you cut off the ends of a roast before cooking it?" a husband asked his wife.

"Because my mother did it that way," she responded.

Curious, the husband called his wife's mother and asked her the same question. When she gave an identical answer, he called his wife's grandmother. The elderly matron laughed and said, "I don't know why *they* cut off the ends of the roast, but I did it that way because a full roast wouldn't fit into my pan."

That story illustrates how most practices are initiated to serve a purpose. But over time, even the best practice can lose its usefulness. It takes a wise leader to know when to change something. Jesus certainly understood the role of change and rebuked those who stood in the way of innovation.

The Pharisees chided Jesus because he didn't force his disciples to fast. Jesus informed them that he had not come to add a few new rules to Judaism. He hadn't come to patch an old system. Such an effort would be as foolish as putting a patch of unshrunk cloth on an old garment, or putting new wine in an old wineskin. When the patch shrunk, the garment would tear. When the wine fermented, the wineskin would burst. The old forms of Judaism could never contain the spirit of Jesus' message.

Jesus was an innovator. A change maker. And so is every effective leader.

If anyone is in Christ, he is a new creation; the old has gone, the new has come!

2 Corinthians 5:17

The day of the Lord will come like a thief. The heavens will disappear with a roar; the elements will be destroyed by fire, and the earth and everything in it will be laid bare. Since everything will be destroyed in this way, what kind of people ought you to be? You ought to live holy and godly lives.

2 Peter 3:10–11

Jesus Christ is the same yesterday and today and forever.

Hebrews 13:8

Change

I will put my laws in their minds and write them on their hearts. I will be their God, and they will be my people. No longer will a man teach his neighbor, or a man his brother, saying, "Know the Lord," because they will all know me, from the least of them to the greatest. For I will forgive their wickedness and will remember their sins no more.

Hebrews 8:10–12

I the Lord do not change. So you, O descendants of Jacob, are not destroyed.

Malachi 3:6

The Father of the heavenly lights . . . .
does not change like shifting shadows.

James 1:17

He who is the Glory of Israel does not lie or change his mind; for he is not a man, that he should change his mind.

1 Samuel 15:29

Whatever was to my profit I now consider loss for the sake of Christ.

Philippians 3:7

God's Words of Life on

Change

God is not a man, that he should lie, nor a son of man, that he should change his mind. Does he speak and then not act? Does he promise and not fulfill?

Numbers 23:19

By dying to what once bound us, we have been released from the law so that we serve in the new way of the Spirit, and not in the old way of the written code.

Romans 7:6

Since, then, you have been raised with Christ, set your hearts on things above, where Christ is seated at the right hand of God. Set your minds on things above, not on earthly things. For you died, and your life is now hidden with Christ in God.

Colossians 3:1–3

You, however, are controlled not by the sinful nature but by the Spirit, if the Spirit of God lives in you.

Romans 8:9

God's Words of Life on

Change

You were taught, with regard to your former way of life, to put off your old self, which is being corrupted by its deceitful desires; to be made new in the attitude of your minds; and to put on the new self, created to be like God in true righteousness and holiness.

Ephesians 4:22–24

When I was a child, I talked like a child, I thought like a child, I reasoned like a child. When I became a man, I put childish ways behind me.

1 Corinthians 13:11

We know that our old self was crucified with him so that the body of sin might be done away with, that we should no longer be slaves to sin —because anyone who has died has been freed from sin.

Romans 6:6–7

Jesus said, "No one sews a patch of unshrunk cloth on an old garment, for the patch will pull away from the garment, making the tear

Change

worse. Neither do men pour new wine into old wineskins. If they do, the skins will burst, the wine will run out and the wineskins will be ruined. No, they pour new wine into new wineskins, and both are preserved."

Matthew 9:16 –17

Behold, I will create new heavens and a new earth. The former things will not be remembered, nor will they come to mind. But be glad and rejoice forever in what I will create, for I will create Jerusalem to be a delight and its people a joy.

Isaiah 65:17 –18

Forget the former things; do not dwell on the past. See, I am doing a new thing! Now it springs up; do you not perceive it? I am making a way in the desert and streams in the wasteland.

Isaiah 43:18 –19

God's Words of Life on
Character

An Inner Reality

The chances are that the common quality in the people you esteem is inward character. Leaders cultivate character by acquiring wisdom and understanding. Of course, those possessions don't come without a price. They require the kind of dedicated and patient labor exercised in mining for gold and silver. As we dig, we must ask God to provide us with insight and understanding. Ultimately, only God can open our eyes to see spiritual truth and then enable us to apply that truth to our lives. As God fills our minds with wisdom, our character will develop so that we'll possess the ability to consistently make right choices —choices that are just, fair and moral.

Where do people with such ideals and insights come from? Character is not a matter of outward technique but of inner reality. People are not impressed by facades or manipulation, but by authenticity and by those who are genuinely other-centered. It's amazing what God can do with a person who wants to grow personally and develop character. The

Character

great news is that God wants us to grow as much as we can. He redeemed us for that purpose. God wants to help us to develop our character.

As we seek to possess God's wisdom, we'll be able to move beyond simply expressing the vision and values of a leader. We'll possess the kind of character from which lofty visions and values flow. Our character will be truly godly, so that others will delight in following us.

What good is it, my brothers, if a man claims to have faith but has no deeds? Can such faith save him? Suppose a brother or sister is without clothes and daily food. If one of you says to him, "Go, I wish you well; keep warm and well fed," but does nothing about his physical needs, what good is it?

James 2:14–16

In everything, do to others what you would have them do to you, for this sums up the Law and the Prophets.

Matthew 7:12

God's Words of Life on

Character

Jesus replied: "'Love the Lord your God with all your heart and with all your soul and with all your mind.' This is the first and greatest commandment. And the second is like it: 'Love your neighbor as yourself.' All the Law and the Prophets hang on these two commandments."

Matthew 22:37–40

The entire law is summed up in a single command: "Love your neighbor as yourself."

Galatians 5:14

Lord, who may dwell in your sanctuary? Who may live on your holy hill? He whose walk is blameless and who does what is righteous, who speaks the truth from his heart and has no slander on his tongue, who does his neighbor no wrong and casts no slur on his fellowman, who despises a vile man but honors those who fear the Lord, who keeps his oath even when it hurts, who lends his money without usury and does not accept a bribe against the innocent. He who does these things will never be shaken.

Psalm 15:1–5

God's Words of Life on

Character

The fruit of the Spirit is love, joy, peace, patience, kindness, goodness, faithfulness, gentleness and self-control. Against such things there is no law.

Galatians 5:22–23

He has showed you, O man, what is good. And what does the Lord require of you? To act justly and to love mercy and to walk humbly with your God.

Micah 6:8

The things that come out of the mouth come from the heart, and these make a man "unclean." For out of the heart come evil thoughts, murder, adultery, sexual immorality, theft, false testimony, slander.

Matthew 15:18–19

Keep falsehood and lies far from me; give me neither poverty nor riches, but give me only my daily bread. Otherwise, I may have too much and disown you and say, "Who is the Lord?" Or I may become poor and steal, and so dishonor the name of my God.

Proverbs 30:8–9

God's Words of Life on

Character

Who may ascend the hill of the LORD? Who may stand in his holy place? He who has clean hands and a pure heart, who does not lift up his soul to an idol or swear by what is false.

PSALM 24:3–4

Better a poor man whose walk is blameless than a rich man whose ways are perverse.

PROVERBS 28:6

We also rejoice in our sufferings, because we know that suffering produces perseverance; perseverance, character; and character, hope.

ROMANS 5:3–4

Be careful that you do not forget the LORD your God, failing to observe his commands, his laws and his decrees that I am giving you this day.

DEUTERONOMY 8:11

If we had forgotten the name of our God or spread out our hands to a foreign god, would not God have discovered it, since he knows the secrets of the heart?

PSALM 44:20–21

God's Words of Life on Commitment

A Deeper Commitment

Quality relationships are founded on the rock of commitment, not the shifting sand of feelings or emotions. Effective leadership flows from commitment to the right things. God calls us to be a people of commitment, first to him and then to others. As followers of Christ, the single most important commitment of our lives is to God. Any true (and eternal) success we experience as leaders will flow from that commitment.

The apostle Paul urges us on God's behalf to devote ourselves to God. In light of God's mercy, which justifies, sanctifies, and will someday glorify us, we are to offer ourselves as living sacrifices to him. In other words, we should allow God's mercy to accomplish this additional work in our lives. We should let it drive us to absolute commitment. At some point we should be motivated by God's mercy to devote ourselves to him. When we take this step, we're acknowledging Christ's leadership in our lives. We sacrifice our selfish desires and misguided ambitions as we strive to align ourselves with God's will. Once this act of commitment occurs, our talents and dreams will be surrendered to his purpose. And the more we give ourselves to him, the more he will bless and use us.

Have you committed yourself completely to Christ? It not, consider doing so now. if you're a devoted follower of Christ, perhaps you could consider renewing this commitment.

Daniel resolved not to defile himself with the royal food and wine, and he asked the chief official for permission not to defile himself this way.

Daniel 1:8

Lord, who may dwell in your sanctuary? Who may live on your holy hill? He whose walk is blameless and who does what is righteous, who speaks the truth from his heart.

Psalm 15:1–2

You have heard that it was said to the people long ago, "Do not break your oath, but keep the oaths you have made to the Lord." But I tell you, Do not swear at all: either by heaven, for it is God's throne; or by the earth, for it is his footstool; or by Jerusalem, for it is the city of the Great King. And do not swear by your head, for you cannot make even one hair white or black. Simply let your "Yes" be "Yes," and your "No," "No"; anything beyond this comes from the evil one.

Matthew 5:33–37

He who swears by heaven swears by God's throne and by the one who sits on it.

Matthew 23:22

Above all, my brothers, do not swear —not by heaven or by earth or by anything else. Let your "Yes" be yes, and your "No," no, or you will be condemned.

James 5:12

Anyone who runs ahead and does not continue in the teaching of Christ does not have God; whoever continues in the teaching has both the Father and the Son.

2 John 9

Do not be yoked together with unbelievers.

GOD'S WORDS OF LIFE ON

COMMITMENT

For what do righteousness and wickedness have in common? Or what fellowship can light have with darkness?

2 CORINTHIANS 6:14

Do not conform any longer to the pattern of this world, but be transformed by the renewing of your mind. Then you will be able to test and approve what God's will is —his good, pleasing and perfect will.

ROMANS 12:2

Jesus said, "Whoever acknowledges me before men, I will also acknowledge him before my Father in heaven. But whoever disowns me before men, I will disown him before my Father in heaven."

MATTHEW 10:32 –33

Samuel replied: "Does the LORD delight in burnt offerings and sacrifices as much as in obeying the voice of the LORD? To obey is better than sacrifice, and to heed is better than the fat of rams."

1 SAMUEL 15:22

God's Words of Life on

Commitment

See, I am setting before you today a blessing and a curse —the blessing if you obey the commands of the LORD your God that I am giving you today; the curse if you disobey the commands of the LORD your God and turn from the way that I command you today by following other gods, which you have not known.

DEUTERONOMY 11:26 –28

If only you had paid attention to my commands, your peace would have been like a river, your righteousness like the waves of the sea.

ISAIAH 48:18

LORD, you establish peace for us; all that we have accomplished you have done for us.

ISAIAH 26:12

I will give them singleness of heart and action, so that they will always fear me for their own good and the good of their children after them. I will make an everlasting covenant with them: I will never stop doing good to them, and I will inspire them to fear me, so that they will never turn away from me.

JEREMIAH 32:39 –40

God's Words of Life on

Communication

Effective Communication

Because we have been created in the likeness of God, we are personal, relational, communicating beings. The issue is not whether we will communicate, but how effective and appropriate our communication will be.

No leader who cannot communicate can lead well or long. Most leaders spend vast amounts of time and energy developing other skills, such as long-term planning, time management and public speaking. But what about taking time to develop the skill of *listening?* Listening, which leads to understanding, is one of the effective leader's best communication strategies. Those who wish to be good leaders will develop this skill. They'll practice such techniques as maintaining eye contact and rephrasing what they hear to be certain that they have understood correctly.

Closely tied in with the skill of listening is the ability to express oneself in a nonabrasive and affirming manner. Our speech can be a source of blessing or injury to others. Wise leaders think before they speak; in so doing they select words that nurture rather than destroy. When faced with hostility they speak gently so as to subdue anger rather than stoke it.

Effective communication involves more than just speaking and hearing. Be on the alert for one-sided communication. Real communication only takes place when both parties move beyond speaking and hearing to understanding. Your degree of ability to communicate will either evoke trust or distrust in those you lead. It will instill either confidence or fear. It will determine to a large extent how eagerly your followers will follow you.

A man finds joy in giving an apt reply —and how good is a timely word!

Proverbs 15:23

The Sovereign Lord has given me an instructed tongue, to know the word that sustains the weary. He wakens me morning by morning, wakens my ear to listen like one being taught.

Isaiah 50:4

God's Words of Life on

Communication

From the fruit of his lips a man is filled with good things as surely as the work of his hands rewards him.

Proverbs 12:14

Do not let any unwholesome talk come out of your mouths, but only what is helpful for building others up according to their needs, that it may benefit those who listen.

Ephesians 4:29

How can you who are evil say anything good? For out of the overflow of the heart the mouth speaks.

Matthew 12:34

Let your conversation be always full of grace, seasoned with salt, so that you may know how to answer everyone.

Colossians 4:6

Nor should there be obscenity, foolish talk or coarse joking, which are out of place, but rather thanksgiving.

Ephesians 5:4

GOD'S WORDS OF LIFE ON

COMMUNICATION

You must rid yourselves of all such things as these: anger, rage, malice, slander, and filthy language from your lips. Do not lie to each other, since you have taken off your old self with its practices

COLOSSIANS 3:8–9

We all stumble in many ways. If anyone is never at fault in what he says, he is a perfect man, able to keep his whole body in check. When we put bits into the mouths of horses to make them obey us, we can turn the whole animal . . . . . Likewise the tongue is a small part of the body, but it makes great boasts. Consider what a great forest is set on fire by a small spark. The tongue also is a fire, a world of evil among the parts of the body. It corrupts the whole person, sets the whole course of his life on fire, and is itself set on fire by hell . . . . . No man can tame the tongue. It is a restless evil, full of deadly poison.

JAMES 3:2–8

An honest answer is like a kiss on the lips.

PROVERBS 24:26

Conflict

Conflict Management

When Jesus addressed problems, he tackled them head-on. While delivering the Sermon on the Mount (and later in Matthew 18) he dealt with the issue of conflicts brought about either by others offending us or by our offending them. No matter which side has caused the problem, the solution is the same: First, go to the person with whom you are experiencing a conflict and address the issues face-to-face. Avoid involving a third or fourth person, especially if their knowledge of the situation will worsen the problem for the offending individual.

Second, go to the person quickly. Jesus counseled that, if someone is worshiping God and remembers that he or she has offended a friend, the appropriate response is to stop right there and go immediately to the offended individual. With those words Jesus made it clear that relational harmony is so important that it must be achieved before effective worship can take place.

Effective leaders don't ignore conflict.

Conflict

They manage it by creating an environment in which people are enabled to work through relational friction on a one-on-one basis. Only after such efforts have failed are others allowed to enter the conflict, and then only for the purpose of bringing about reconciliation. Conflicts can't be avoided. But they can be managed. And a wise leader will devote himself or herself to learning how to do that.

Do not be overcome by evil, but overcome evil with good.

Romans 12:21

May the God who gives endurance and encouragement give you a spirit of unity among yourselves as you follow Christ Jesus, so that with one heart and mouth you may glorify the God and Father of our Lord Jesus Christ. Accept one another, then, just as Christ accepted you, in order to bring praise to God.

Romans 15:5–7

God's Words of Life on

Conflict

I appeal to you, brothers, in the name of our Lord Jesus Christ, that all of you agree with one another so that there may be no divisions among you and that you may be perfectly united in mind and thought.

1 Corinthians 1:10

Whatever happens, conduct yourselves in a manner worthy of the gospel of Christ. Then, whether I come and see you or only hear about you in my absence, I will know that you stand firm in one spirit, contending as one man for the faith of the gospel.

Philippians 1:27

Make my joy complete by being like-minded, having the same love, being one in spirit and purpose. Do nothing out of selfish ambition or vain conceit, but in humility consider others better than yourselves. Each of you should look not only to your own interests, but also to the interests of others.

Philippians 2:2–4

Let us therefore make every effort to do what leads to peace and to mutual edification.

Romans 14:19

God's Words of Life on

Conflict

Live in harmony with one another; be sympathetic, love as brothers, be compassionate and humble. Do not repay evil with evil or insult with insult, but with blessing, because to this you were called so that you may inherit a blessing.

1 Peter 3:8–9

Do not hate your brother in your heart. Rebuke your neighbor frankly so you will not share in his guilt. Do not seek revenge or bear a grudge against one of your people, but love your neighbor as yourself. I am the Lord.

Leviticus 19:17–18

Then the Lord said to Cain, "Why are you angry? Why is your face downcast? If you do what is right, will you not be accepted? But if you do not do what is right, sin is crouching at your door; it desires to have you, but you must master it."

Genesis 4:6–7

Refrain from anger and turn from wrath; do not fret—it leads only to evil.

Psalm 37:8

God's Words of Life on

Conflict

A fool shows his annoyance at once, but a prudent man overlooks an insult.

Proverbs 12:16

A gentle answer turns away wrath, but a harsh word stirs up anger.

Proverbs 15:1

A hot-tempered man stirs up dissension, but a patient man calms a quarrel.

Proverbs 15:8

Starting a quarrel is like breaching a dam; so drop the matter before a dispute breaks out.

Proverbs 17:14

A man's wisdom gives him patience; it is to his glory to overlook an offense.

Proverbs 19:11

A hot-tempered man must pay the penalty; if you rescue him, you will have to do it again.

Proverbs 19:19

God's Words of Life on

Conflict

Do not make friends with a hot-tempered man, do not associate with one easily angered, or you may learn his ways and get yourself ensnared.

Proverbs 22:24–25

Like a city whose walls are broken down is a man who lacks self-control.

Proverbs 25:28

Get rid of all bitterness, rage and anger, brawling and slander, along with every form of malice. Be kind and compassionate to one another, forgiving each other, just as in Christ God forgave you.

Ephesians 4:31–32

An angry man stirs up dissension, and a hot-tempered one commits many sins.

Proverbs 29:22

For as churning the milk produces butter, and as twisting the nose produces blood, so stirring up anger produces strife.

Proverbs 30:33

Courage

Courage in Crisis

Leaders need courage to make the tough decisions they're faced with every day. From time to time, good leadership requires excursions into unexplored territory, and draws on a leader's courage. Joshua certainly faced such a crisis in his leadership role. Not only did he have to contend with the military powers rooted in the promised land, but he also had to face them with an untrained band of nomadic shepherds.

God realized Joshua's need for courage and gave him guidance that would strengthen his faith. He reminded Joshua of his faithfulness to keep all of his promises. Joshua's success didn't rest on a military strategy or well-trained army, but on the faithfulness of God. The "Book of the Law" would give the wisdom and encouragement Joshua would need to courageously lead the nation. And no matter how intimidating the enemy or how rebellious the people, Joshua would not have to face them alone. God would always be at his side.

The same sources of courage that empowered Joshua are available today for any leader who will accept them. When faced with a risky business decision, the godly leader will look to God in prayer and to God's revealed Word for the perspective and courage needed to make the right choice. What situation are you now facing that requires courageous leadership? Let God's words to Joshua supply you with the courage you need.

The LORD is my light and my salvation — whom shall I fear? The LORD is the stronghold of my life —of whom shall I be afraid?

PSALM 27:1

Do not fear, for I am with you; do not be dismayed, for I am your God. I will strengthen you and help you; I will uphold you with my righteous right hand.

ISAIAH 41:10

Have I not commanded you? Be strong and courageous. Do not be terrified; do not be discouraged, for the LORD your God will be with you wherever you go.

JOSHUA 1:9

God's Words of Life on

Courage

Dear friends, do not be surprised at the painful trial you are suffering, as though something strange were happening to you. But rejoice that you participate in the sufferings of Christ, so that you may be overjoyed when his glory is revealed.

1 Peter 4:12–13

When you pass through the waters, I will be with you; and when you pass through the rivers, they will not sweep over you. When you walk through the fire, you will not be burned; the flames will not set you ablaze.

Isaiah 43:2

In all these things we are more than conquerors through him who loved us. For I am convinced that neither death nor life, neither angels nor demons, neither the present nor the future, nor any powers, neither height nor depth, nor anything else in all creation, will be able to separate us from the love of God that is in Christ Jesus our Lord.

Romans 8:37–39

God's Words of Life on

Courage

Wait for the LORD; be strong and take heart and wait for the LORD.

PSALM 27:14

Be strong and take heart, all you who hope in the LORD.

PSALM 31:24

He gives strength to the weary and increases the power of the weak. Even youths grow tired and weary, and young men stumble and fall; but those who hope in the LORD will renew their strength. They will soar on wings like eagles; they will run and not grow weary, they will walk and not be faint.

ISAIAH 40:29–31

I can do everything through him who gives me strength.

PHILIPPIANS 4:13

Strengthen the feeble hands, steady the knees that give way; say to those with fearful hearts, "Be strong, do not fear; your God will come, he will come with vengeance."

ISAIAH 35:3–4

God's Words of Life on
Courage

Do not be anxious about anything, but in everything, by prayer and petition, with thanksgiving, present your requests to God. And the peace of God, which transcends all understanding, will guard your hearts and your minds in Christ Jesus. Finally, brothers, whatever is true, whatever is noble, whatever is right, whatever is pure, whatever is lovely, whatever is admirable —if anything is excellent or praiseworthy —think about such things.

Philippians 4:6 –8

I have prayed for you, Simon, that your faith may not fail. And when you have turned back, strengthen your brothers.

Luke 22:32

Be strong and very courageous. Be careful to obey all the law my servant Moses gave you; do not turn from it to the right or to the left, that you may be successful wherever you go.

Joshua 1:7

Decision Making

Big or Small, Make Them All with God

Decision making is one of leadership's core competencies. Decisions reveal values and intelligence. They require obedience to and dependence upon God. As your mind scans the topics related to leadership, it will become apparent that making decisions affects just about everything else leaders do. In a given day, the decisions can number into the thousands. Some are small; others are life altering.

Where can a leader go to get help in this essential component of life and leadership? Of all the Bible's leaders, Nehemiah provides one of our best patterns for "doing it right." Nehemiah was effective in this essential leadership task.

Nehemiah was faced with a huge challenge: The walls of Jerusalem were in disrepair, and the returned exiles were vulnerable and disheartened. Nehemiah carefully studied the situation. He empathized with those who were hurting. He humbled himself before God. And Nehemiah prayed! Nehemiah adored God, confessed his nation's sin to the Lord and finally petitioned God for help.

Ultimately, Nehemiah knew what every great leader knows: Decision makers must understand complicated matters, but they also need God's perspective in deciding how to act. All wisdom comes from God. Using his wisdom to make good decisions is something God wants to help us learn to do. We make decisions every day, and the patterns established by the small decisions shape the course of the larger ones. It's crucial to make wise decisions, but no decision is wise if it's made independently of God.

He who answers before listening —that is his folly and his shame.

PROVERBS 18:13

This is the confidence we have in approaching God: that if we ask anything according to his will, he hears us.

1 JOHN 5:14

The heart of the discerning acquires knowledge; the ears of the wise seek it out.

PROVERBS 18:15

God's Words of Life on

Decision Making

If any of you lacks wisdom, he should ask God, who gives generously to all without finding fault, and it will be given to him. But when he asks, he must believe and not doubt, because he who doubts is like a wave of the sea, blown and tossed by the wind.

James 1:5–6

You have known the holy Scriptures, which are able to make you wise for salvation through faith in Christ Jesus.

2 Timothy 3:15

Buy the truth and do not sell it; get wisdom, discipline and understanding.

Proverbs 23:23

Give your servant a discerning heart to govern your people and to distinguish between right and wrong.

1 Kings 3:9

The discerning heart seeks knowledge, but the mouth of a fool feeds on folly.

Proverbs 15:14

God's Words of Life on

Decision Making

Wise men store up knowledge, but the mouth of a fool invites ruin.

Proverbs 10:14

Your commands make me wiser than my enemies, for they are ever with me. I have more insight than all my teachers, for I meditate on your statutes. I have more understanding than the elders, for I obey your precepts.

Psalm 119:98–100

Instruct a wise man and he will be wiser still; teach a righteous man and he will add to his learning.

Proverbs 9:9

Get wisdom, get understanding; do not forget my words or swerve from them. Do not forsake wisdom, and she will protect you; love her, and she will watch over you. Wisdom is supreme; therefore get wisdom. Though it cost all you have, get understanding.

Proverbs 4:5–7

God's Words of Life on

Dependence on God

Lean on Him

All people who lead others or carry organizational responsibility find more than enough reasons to worry —deadlines, financial pressures, market instability and other pressures make stomachs churn and account for many a sleepless night. But Jesus cautions us against worrying about anything —even the food we eat or the clothes we wear. In Matthew 6, Jesus gives his disciples (and us) six reasons for trusting in God rather than worrying.

First, the same God who gives us the greater gift of life will certainly supply the lesser gifts of food and clothing. Second, the God who cares for birds will care for his people. Third, worry expends energy pointlessly —it doesn't change the reality of the situation a single bit. Fourth, worry ignores God's demonstrated faithfulness in our lives. Fifth, we are God's children. God will never treat us as orphans who need to fend for themselves. Sixth, when we worry about tomorrow we miss out on today. Any problem we face can be handled, with God's help, one day at a time.

God's Words of Life on

Dependence on God

As leaders who want to impact our generation for Christ, we need to lead in a way that allows others to see our faith in God. One way we can do that is by depending on God in the face of our daily pressures. The next time you're under pressure, pray for the grace you need to depend on God. Those you lead will see how you respond to such pressures and will follow your actions.

Those who know your name will trust in you, for you, LORD, have never forsaken those who seek you.

PSALM 9:10

He did not waver through unbelief regarding the promise of God, but was strengthened in his faith and gave glory to God, being fully persuaded that God had power to do what he had promised.

ROMANS 4:20–21

Taste and see that the LORD is good; blessed is the man who takes refuge in him.

PSALM 34:8

God's Words of Life on

Dependence on God

O Lord Almighty, blessed is the man who trusts in you.

Psalm 84:12

Those who trust in the Lord are like Mount Zion, which cannot be shaken but endures forever.

Psalm 125:1

Blessed is he whose help is the God of Jacob, whose hope is in the Lord his God.

Psalm 146:5

Whoever gives heed to instruction prospers, and blessed is he who trusts in the Lord.

Proverbs 16:20

Blessed is the man who trusts in the Lord, whose confidence is in him. He will be like a tree planted by the water that sends out its roots by the stream. It does not fear when heat comes; its leaves are always green. It has no worries in a year of drought and never fails to bear fruit.

Jeremiah 17:7–8

God's Words of Life on

Dependence on God

You will keep in perfect peace him whose mind is steadfast, because he trusts in you. Trust in the LORD forever, for the LORD, the LORD, is the Rock eternal.

ISAIAH 26:3–4

The LORD longs to be gracious to you; he rises to show you compassion. For the LORD is a God of justice. Blessed are all who wait for him!

ISAIAH 30:18

Hezekiah trusted in the LORD, the God of Israel. There was no one like him among all the kings of Judah, either before him or after him.

2 KINGS 18:5

Many are the woes of the wicked, but the LORD's unfailing love surrounds the man who trusts in him.

PSALM 32:10

Trust in the LORD and do good; dwell in the land and enjoy safe pasture.

PSALM 37:3

God's Words of Life on

Double-Loop Learning

A Second Time Around

Leaders have to address issues of heart and soul that determine how and why problematic behavior is being practiced. Jesus modeled this essential discipline of effective leadership. Peter had failed Jesus miserably. Overwhelmed by intense pressure, he had abandoned his mentor and friend in the moment Jesus most needed his friendship and support. How humiliated and degraded Peter must have felt. But Jesus reconstructed Peter.

He could have delivered a lecture on commitment. He didn't. Jesus didn't address Peter's behavior at all; he knew he didn't have to. Rather, Jesus penetrated to the heart of the problem. He realized that good behavior grows out of a good heart. Jesus practiced what Chris Argyris calls "double-loop learning." Three times Jesus forced Peter to examine the root cause of his problem. While Peter's behavioral problem was important, Jesus knew that a change wouldn't last unless the root of the behavior was addressed.

The single loop tends to be the easy one. We can teach a person to modify his or her

Double-Loop Learning

angry outbursts. But the second loop forces the person to deal with the anger that generates the outburst. The second loop is essential to solving the problem but more difficult to address.

As a leader who is committed to God's best for your followers, learn well the lesson of double-loop learning. First time around the loop —behavior. Second time around the loop —values and attitudes that drive behavior. Great leaders don't stop after one lap around the loop.

Jesus said, "Those whom I love I rebuke and discipline. So be earnest, and repent."

Revelation 3:19

Your attitude should be the same as that of Christ Jesus.

Philippians 2:5

Follow my example, as I follow the example of Christ.

1 Corinthians 11:1

God's Words of Life on

Double-Loop Learning

I try to please everybody in every way. For I am not seeking my own good but the good of many, so that they may be saved.

1 Corinthians 10:33

Search me, O God, and know my heart; test me and know my anxious thoughts. See if there is any offensive way in me, and lead me in the way everlasting.

Psalm 139:23–24

I the Lord search the heart and examine the mind, to reward a man according to his conduct, according to what his deeds deserve.

Jeremiah 17:10

He who trusts in himself is a fool, but he who walks in wisdom is kept safe.

Proverbs 28:26

See to it that no one misses the grace of God and that no bitter root grows up to cause trouble and defile many.

Hebrews 12:15

God's Words of Life on

Double-Loop Learning

The crucible for silver and the furnace for gold, but the Lord tests the heart.

Proverbs 17:3

O Lord, you have searched me and you know me. You know when I sit and when I rise; you perceive my thoughts from afar.

Psalm 139:1–2

Test me, O Lord, and try me, examine my heart and my mind.

Psalm 26:2

Who can discern his errors? Forgive my hidden faults.

Psalm 19:12

My conscience is clear, but that does not make me innocent. It is the Lord who judges me.

1 Corinthians 4:4

Teach me, and I will be quiet; show me where I have been wrong.

Job 6:24

God's Words of Life on

Double-Loop Learning

You have set our iniquities before you, our secret sins in the light of your presence.

Psalm 90:8

Even if I caused you sorrow by my letter, I do not regret it. Though I did regret it —I see that my letter hurt you, but only for a little while —yet now I am happy, not because you were made sorry, but because your sorrow led you to repentance. For you became sorrowful as God intended and so were not harmed in any way by us. Godly sorrow brings repentance that leads to salvation and leaves no regret, but worldly sorrow brings death. See what this godly sorrow has produced in you: what earnestness, what eagerness to clear yourselves, what indignation, what alarm, what longing, what concern, what readiness to see justice done. At every point you have proved yourselves to be innocent.

2 Corinthians 7:8 –11

God's Words of Life on Empowerment

The Power to Succeed

When Jesus commissioned his disciples to reach the world with his message in Matthew 28, he provided helpful principles for empowerment: Jesus commissioned them to use his power for specific purposes, which he clearly defined. He assured them that he would be there to back them up. He prepared them before delegating the authority to them. He held them accountable for how they used his power.

Then he gave them the power needed to succeed. He promised them the Holy Spirit, who would work through them to achieve God's plan. The disciples also enjoyed the assurance that Jesus stood behind them all the way, supporting them and providing what they needed for the task ahead. By promising to supply what they needed in order to succeed, Jesus empowered his followers.

Leaders can't literally confer power upon others. Delegating authority without resources does not automatically empower others. Leaders can, however, supply the resources and create the conditions that allow people to develop the power they need to do their jobs. Effective leaders think in terms of "enablement" and "freedom" in order to empower their followers.

Jesus invested time and energy developing these leaders. Only at the point at which they could properly manage the resource did Jesus empower them. The leader who offers empowerment too early sets up followers for failure. On the other hand, the leader who fails to empower capable people creates frustration. Are you following Jesus' principles of empowerment?

Jesus said, "Anyone who has faith in me will do what I have been doing. He will do even greater things than these, because I am going to the Father."

JOHN 14:12

Christ told his disciples, "I have given you authority to trample on snakes and scorpions and to overcome all the power of the enemy; nothing will harm you."

LUKE 10:19

God's Words of Life on

Empowerment

Jesus said, "I will give you the keys of the kingdom of heaven; whatever you bind on earth will be bound in heaven, and whatever you loose on earth will be loosed in heaven."

Matthew 16:19

When you are assembled in the name of our Lord Jesus and I am with you in spirit, and the power of our Lord Jesus is present.

1 Corinthians 5:4

The bolts of your gates will be iron and bronze, and your strength will equal your days.

Deuteronomy 33:25

The Lord gives strength to his people; the Lord blesses his people with peace.

Psalm 29:11

Jesus said, "I tell you the truth, whatever you bind on earth will be bound in heaven, and whatever you loose on earth will be loosed in heaven."

Matthew 18:18

God's Words of Life on

Empowerment

The LORD told his people, "Do not fear, for I am with you; do not be dismayed, for I am your God. I will strengthen you and help you; I will uphold you with my righteous right hand."

Isaiah 41:10

He said to me, "My grace is sufficient for you, for my power is made perfect in weakness." Therefore I will boast all the more gladly about my weaknesses, so that Christ's power may rest on me. That is why, for Christ's sake, I delight in weaknesses, in insults, in hardships, in persecutions, in difficulties. For when I am weak, then I am strong.

2 Corinthians 12:9–10

I can do everything through God who gives me strength.

Philippians 4:13

The LORD bless you and keep you; the LORD make his face shine upon you and be gracious to you; the LORD turn his face toward you and give you peace.

Numbers 6:24–26

God's Words of Life on

Empowerment

Being strengthened with all power according to his glorious might so that you may have great endurance and patience, and joyfully giving thanks to the Father, who has qualified you to share in the inheritance of the saints in the kingdom of light.

COLOSSIANS 1:11–12

The LORD is the strength of his people, a fortress of salvation for his anointed one.

PSALM 28:8

In the LORD alone are righteousness and strength.

ISAIAH 45:24

I pray that out of his glorious riches he may strengthen you with power through his Spirit in your inner being, so that Christ may dwell in your hearts through faith.

EPHESIANS 3:16–17

You are awesome, O God, in your sanctuary; the God of Israel gives power and strength to his people. Praise be to God!

PSALM 68:35

GOD'S WORDS OF LIFE ON

EMPOWERMENT

They go from strength to strength, till each appears before God in Zion.

PSALM 84:7

Those who hope in the LORD will renew their strength. They will soar on wings like eagles; they will run and not grow weary, they will walk and not be faint.

ISAIAH 40:31

"I will strengthen them in the LORD and in his name they will walk," declares the LORD.

ZECHARIAH 10:12

Wealth and honor come from you; you are the ruler of all things. In your hands are strength and power to exalt and give strength to all.

1 CHRONICLES 29:12

Nevertheless, the righteous will hold to their ways, and those with clean hands will grow stronger.

JOB 17:9

He gives strength to the weary and increases the power of the weak.

ISAIAH 40:29

Encouragement

The Benefits of Encouragement

Few functions a leader performs are more important than that of keeping hope alive. During those times in which others are lost in a dark and seemingly endless maze of despair, effective leaders will drive away the darkness with positive projections for the future. They'll infuse those around them with optimism regarding themselves, others and the future of the organization. They know when to draw alongside of someone. They sense whether a team member needs a quick admonition or a shoulder on which to cry.

No other New Testament character illustrates the ability to encourage more strongly than Barnabas, whose name means "Son of Encouragement." The disciples in Jerusalem were understandably afraid of Saul. Based upon his reputation for zealotry and cruelty, it's no wonder that they questioned the validity of his profession of faith in Christ. As a devout Pharisee, Saul had doggedly hunted down and persecuted followers of Jesus.

ENCOURAGEMENT

Due to this suspicion, it seemed that Saul's ministry would flounder before it ever got started. And that might have happened had not Barnabas stood in the gap beside Saul, leading him to the apostles and testifying concerning his conversion and subsequent ministry. Barnabas encouraged the apostles to bless Saul's ministry, and they responded favorably. Barnabas provided the timely support that Saul needed to launch his ministry.

Effective leaders, like Barnabas, sustain hope by offering words of support. And a little bit of encouragement can go a long way toward motivating those around you too.

I will remember the deeds of the LORD; yes, I will remember your miracles of long ago. I will meditate on all your works and consider all your mighty deeds.

PSALM 77:11–12

You, O LORD, are a compassionate and gracious God, slow to anger, abounding in love and faithfulness.

PSALM 86:15

God's Words of Life on

Encouragement

In your great mercy you did not put an end to them or abandon them, for you are a gracious and merciful God.

Nehemiah 9:31

Who is a God like you, who pardons sin and forgives the transgression of the remnant of his inheritance? You do not stay angry forever but delight to show mercy. You will again have compassion on us; you will tread our sins underfoot and hurl all our iniquities into the depths of the sea.

Micah 7:18–19

Do not gloat over me, my enemy! Though I have fallen, I will rise. Though I sit in darkness, the Lord will be my light.

Micah 7:8

His mercy extends to those who fear him, from generation to generation.

Luke 1:50

He who trusts in himself is a fool, but he who walks in wisdom is kept safe.

Proverbs 28:26

God's Words of Life on

Encouragement

Yet this I call to mind and therefore I have hope: Because of the Lord's great love we are not consumed, for his compassions never fail. They are new every morning; great is your faithfulness.

LAMENTATIONS 3:21–23

God, who has called you into fellowship with his Son Jesus Christ our Lord, is faithful.

1 CORINTHIANS 1:9

Commit to the LORD whatever you do, and your plans will succeed

PROVERBS 16:3

The LORD is good to those whose hope is in him, to the one who seeks him.

LAMENTATIONS 3:25

An anxious heart weighs a man down, but a kind word cheers him up.

PROVERBS 12:25

My mouth would encourage you; comfort from my lips would bring you relief.

JOB 16:5

Excellence

Pursue Excellence

There are dangers to compromising excellence. NBA players and coaches are committed to excellence because they want to win a championship. Corporate executives are committed to excellence because they want to please their customers and increase profits. These can be good motives. But as followers of Christ the motive that drives us to excellence should be a desire to please the one who will give us our final reward. Everything we do should be done with a conscious awareness of his presence, a realization that he is watching.

Such awareness should prompt us, regardless of our field of endeavor, to give our best effort all of the time, knowing that there is never a circumstance during which the one we follow is not with us, urging us on to our finest.

It's easy to expect and demand excellence from those we lead. But where does excellence from our followers find its inspiration? Psalm 78:72 lays the responsibility squarely back upon the leader's shoulders. It is one thing to speak about excellence and another to pursue it. We often long for more but settle for less,

Excellence

falling prey to the inertia of sloppy habits and mediocre routines. Strive for excellence in all you do. God certainly exhibits it in his character and deeds. Quality is important.

Jesus said, "Remain in me, and I will remain in you. No branch can bear fruit by itself; it must remain in the vine. Neither can you bear fruit unless you remain in me. I am the vine; you are the branches. If a man remains in me and I in him, he will bear much fruit; apart from me you can do nothing."

John 15:4–5

Forgetting what is behind and straining toward what is ahead, I press on toward the goal to win the prize for which God has called me heavenward in Christ Jesus.

Philippians 3:13–14

Do you not know that in a race all the runners run, but only one gets the prize? Run in such a way as to get the prize.

1 Corinthians 9:24

God's Words of Life on

Excellence

Since we are surrounded by such a great cloud of witnesses, let us throw off everything that hinders and the sin that so easily entangles, and let us run with perseverance the race marked out for us.

Hebrews 12:1

No one who puts his hand to the plow and looks back is fit for service in the kingdom of God.

Luke 9:62

We are therefore Christ's ambassadors, as though God were making his appeal through us. We implore you on Christ's behalf: Be reconciled to God.

1 Corinthians 5:20

I consider everything a loss compared to the surpassing greatness of knowing Christ Jesus my Lord, for whose sake I have lost all things. I consider them rubbish, that I may gain Christ.

Philippians 3:8

God's Words of Life on

Excellence

I press on to take hold of that for which Christ Jesus took hold of me.

Philippians 3:12

I know what it is to be in need, and I know what it is to have plenty. I have learned the secret of being content in any and every situation, whether well fed or hungry, whether living in plenty or in want.

Philippians 4:12

I consider my life worth nothing to me, if only I may finish the race and complete the task the Lord Jesus has given me —the task of testifying to the gospel of God's grace.

Acts 20:24

Make it your ambition to lead a quiet life, to mind your own business and to work with your hands, just as we told you, so that your daily life may win the respect of outsiders and so that you will not be dependent on anybody.

1 Thessalonians 4:11 –12

God's Words of Life on

Excellence

I have fought the good fight, I have finished the race, I have kept the faith.

2 Timothy 4:7

Then I heard the voice of the Lord saying, "Whom shall I send? And who will go for us?" And I said, "Here am I. Send me!"

Isaiah 6:8

Do not be afraid of those who kill the body but cannot kill the soul. Rather, be afraid of the One who can destroy both soul and body in hell.

Matthew 10:28

Whoever wants to save his life will lose it, but whoever loses his life for me will find it.

Matthew 16:25

The man who loves his life will lose it, while the man who hates his life in this world will keep it for eternal life.

John 12:25

God's Words of Life on

Exhortation

Effective Exhortation

Leadership is an art consisting of skills that can be studied, practiced and mastered. Effective leaders may be found in the boardroom and in the boiler room. They may be teachers, coaches, bankers, lawyers, service station attendants or food servers. Among the relational skills effective leaders cultivate is that of exhortation. Exhorters are people who spur others on to higher levels of achievement. In doing so, they help turn their constituents into leaders. Effective leaders accomplish extraordinary things by enabling others to act.

The apostle Paul demonstrated this ability in 2 Timothy 2:14 –21. Paul began with a general exhortation for Timothy to present himself to God "as one approved" (v. 15). He then offered specific guidelines as to how Timothy could accomplish this through his study and teaching of God's Word. Finally, Paul offered a negative illustration followed by a positive one: Timothy was not to be like Hymenaus and Philetus, who had strayed from the truth. Instead, he was to be like a gold vessel in a great house. That vessel,

Exhortation

when kept clean and polished, would be used by the Master for a noble purpose.

Effective leaders use a variety of communication techniques to exhort those around them to strive for higher levels of performance. We know that, through Paul's exhortation and the Spirit's work in his life, Timothy became a great leader in the early church. Is there someone you know who might be spurred on to great things as a result of your exhortation?

Do not rebuke an older man harshly, but exhort him as if he were your father. Treat younger men as brothers.

1 Timothy 5:1

Give everyone what you owe him: If you owe taxes, pay taxes; if revenue, then revenue; if respect, then respect; if honor, then honor.

Romans 13:7

If someone is caught in a sin, you who are spiritual should restore him gently. But watch yourself, or you also may be tempted.

Galatians 6:1

God's Words of Life on

Exhortation

Be merciful to those who doubt; snatch others from the fire and save them.

Jude 22–23

If anyone sees his brother commit a sin that does not lead to death, he should pray and God will give him life.

1 John 5:16

If one of you should wander from the truth and someone should bring him back, remember this: Whoever turns a sinner from the error of his way will save him from death and cover over a multitude of sins.

James 5:19–20

Jesus told Peter, "I have prayed for you . . . . that your faith may not fail. And when you have turned back, strengthen your brothers."

Luke 22:32

The Lord declared, "I will search for the lost and bring back the strays. I will bind up the injured and strengthen the weak."

Ezekiel 34:16

God's Words of Life on

Exhortation

Strengthen the feeble hands, steady the knees that give way; say to those with fearful hearts, "Be strong, do not fear; your God will come, he will come with vengeance; with divine retribution he will come to save you."

Isaiah 35:3–4

Think how you have instructed many, how you have strengthened feeble hands. Your words have supported those who stumbled; you have strengthened faltering knees.

Job 4:3–4

The Lord's servant must not quarrel; instead, he must be kind to everyone, able to teach, not resentful. Those who oppose him he must gently instruct, in the hope that God will grant them repentance.

2 Timothy 2:24–25

Peacemakers who sow in peace raise a harvest of righteousness.

James 3:18

Friendships & Alliances

The Strength of Alliances

A story is told about a boy who valiantly, but unsuccessfully, attempted to move a heavy log. His dad stood quietly nearby, watching his son straining against the load. Finally he said, "Son, why aren't you using all of your strength?"

Confused and a little angry, the boy responded, "Dad, I'm using every last little bit of strength I have!"

"No, son, you're not," his dad quietly responded. "You haven't asked me to help."

Effective leaders use all of their strength by recognizing, developing and utilizing the people around them. They know how to develop healthy alliances both with those on their own team and those on other teams.

While fleeing from Saul, David certainly demonstrated that ability. While he was in hiding with his family, David attracted to himself others who were also experiencing hardship. In fact, four hundred men eventually allied themselves with David. In addition to those alliances, David connected with the king of Moab, who provided shelter for his parents.

David possessed the foresight to know that he couldn't go it alone. He worked to build others' trust in his leadership ability, and he evidently proved himself. David's forces were loyal to him, and together they realized success against the enemies of Israel.

Effective leaders possess the unique ability to build alliances with people who can help to advance their causes. What alliances do you now have that are mutually beneficial? What do you do to foster them and to encourage their growth?

A friend loves at all times, and a brother is born for adversity.

Proverbs 17:17

Jesus said, "Greater love has no one than this, that he lay down his life for his friends. You are my friends if you do what I command. I no longer call you servants, because a servant does not know his master's business. Instead, I have called you friends, for everything that I learned from my Father I have made known to you."

John 15:13–15

God's Words of Life on

Friendships & Alliances

A despairing man should have the devotion of his friends.

Job 6:14

He who covers over an offense promotes love, but whoever repeats the matter separates close friends.

Proverbs 17:9

A man of many companions may come to ruin, but there is a friend who sticks closer than a brother.

Proverbs 18:24

My intercessor is my friend as my eyes pour out tears to God.

Job 16:20

Two are better than one, because they have a good return for their work: If one falls down, his friend can help him up. But pity the man who falls and has no one to help him up!

Ecclesiastes 4:9–10

God's Words of Life on

Friendships & Alliances

Do not make friends with a hot-tempered man, do not associate with one easily angered, or you may learn his ways and get yourself ensnared.

Proverbs 22:24–25

Wounds from a friend can be trusted, but an enemy multiplies kisses.

Proverbs 27:6

How good and pleasant it is when brothers live together in unity!

Psalm 133:1

Rejoice with those who rejoice; mourn with those who mourn. Live in harmony with one another. Do not be proud, but be willing to associate with people of low position. Do not be conceited.

Romans 12:15–16

If we walk in the light, as God is in the light, we have fellowship with one another.

1 John 1:7

God's Words of Life on

Human Resources

Managing Human Resources God's Way

How human resource development actually works in everyday life is one of the thorniest areas of leadership. Some of the loudest proclamations of our values are made in the human resource arena.

Since God created us, he knows our aptitudes and abilities better than we do ourselves. Since God loves us, he wants us to move toward the fulfillment of our potential. But we cannot do this without personal commitment to the centrality of Christ in our lives. According to the apostle Paul, the risen Christ himself endowed each believer with unique spiritual gifts, and, in addition, he gave the church special individuals whom he had particularly gifted for spiritual leadership.

Paul emphasized Christ's authority to distribute these gifts. Jesus ascended into heaven and gave special gifts to his people in order to enhance the building of his church. Of course, he didn't impart those gifts merely for the enjoyment of the recipients. Jesus gifted people so that they could exercise these abilities in a way that would bring glory to him and enjoyment and satisfaction to his people.

Jesus beautifully planned that those works of service, performed by his own people, would build up the body of Christ. When we build the lives of others and participate in the development of their potential, we are acting as faithful stewards of our divine responsibilities. What a wonderful use of the gifts of leaders —to help themselves and others attain the fullness of Christ!

Christ said, "He who receives you receives me, and he who receives me receives the one who sent me."

MATTHEW 10:40

How good and pleasant it is when brothers live together in unity!

PSALM 133:1

Do to others as you would have them do to you.

LUKE 6:31

God's Words of Life on

Human Resources

Jesus said, "Give to the one who asks you, and do not turn away from the one who wants to borrow from you. You have heard that it was said, 'Love your neighbor and hate your enemy.' But I tell you: Love your enemies and pray for those who persecute you."

Matthew 5:42–44

To love the Lord with all your heart, with all your understanding and with all your strength, and to love your neighbor as yourself is more important than all burnt offerings and sacrifices.

Mark 12:33

Jesus said, "I tell you the truth, anyone who gives you a cup of water in my name because you belong to Christ will certainly not lose his reward."

Mark 9:41

Jesus told his disciples, "I have set you an example that you should do as I have done for you."

John 13:15

God's Words of Life on

Human Resources

Be devoted to one another in brotherly love. Honor one another above yourselves.

Romans 12:10

May the Lord make your love increase and overflow for each other and for everyone else, just as ours does for you.

1 Thessalonians 3:12

Let us consider how we may spur one another on toward love and good deeds.

Hebrews 10:24

If you really keep the royal law found in Scripture, "Love your neighbor as yourself," you are doing right.

James 2:8

Above all, love each other deeply, because love covers over a multitude of sins.

1 Peter 4:8

God has shown me that I should not call any man impure or unclean.

Acts 10:28

God's Words of Life on

Human Resources

Whoever hates his brother is in the darkness and walks around in the darkness; he does not know where he is going, because the darkness has blinded him.

1 John 2:11

Dear friends, let us love one another, for love comes from God. Everyone who loves has been born of God and knows God.

1 John 4:7

The Lord himself is our peace, who has made the two one and has destroyed the barrier, the dividing wall of hostility.

Ephesians 2:14

You have been given fullness in Christ, who is the head over every power and authority.

Colossians 2:10

When you were dead in your sins and in the uncircumcision of your sinful nature, God made you alive with Christ.

Colossians 2:13

God's Words of Life on
Human Resources

The body is a unit, though it is made up of many parts; and though all its parts are many, they form one body.

1 Corinthians 12:12

There is neither Jew nor Greek, slave nor free, male nor female, for you are all one in Christ Jesus.

Galatians 3:28

Make room for us in your hearts. We have wronged no one, we have corrupted no one, we have exploited no one.

2 Corinthians 7:2

I have filled him with the Spirit of God, with skill, ability and knowledge in all kinds of crafts.

Exodus 31:3

I have given skill to all the craftsmen to make everything I have commanded you.

Exodus 31:6

Humility

Reflection of Strength

The main goal for godly leaders is to reflect the life of Christ in their own lives. And the character trait that best enables us to do that is humility. In his earthly life, Christ himself was the perfect exemplar of true humility.

First, Jesus didn't selfishly cling to the outer expression of his divinity. Jesus didn't come as a king, but as a helpless infant. Although he was perfectly God and perfectly human at the same time (John 1:14), he took the form of a servant. A humble leader doesn't flaunt his or her position or power. Instead, he or she identifies with the weakest member of the team. Second, Jesus demonstrated humility through obedience to God the Father. A humble leader doesn't impose his or her will on God, but submits to God's commands. Third, Jesus waited for his Father to lift him up. A humble leader doesn't grab for power or position. He or she patiently waits for God to increase his or her influence.

Humility has fallen on hard times. Contrary to popular opinion, humility is not a matter of

Humility

weakness or passivity; from a Biblical point of view, it is disciplined strength and other-centered power. The problem with the virtue of humility is that as soon as we think we have attained it, we have lost it. Jesus set the perfect example of humility. Follow Jesus' example as you seek to demonstrate the kind of humility that will cause others to see Jesus in you.

All of you, clothe yourselves with humility toward one another, because, "God opposes the proud but gives grace to the humble." Humble yourselves, therefore, under God's mighty hand, that he may lift you up in due time.

1 Peter 5:5–6

As God's chosen people, holy and dearly loved, clothe yourselves with compassion, kindness, humility, gentleness and patience.

Colossians 3:12

The Lord said, "I live in a high and holy place, but also with him who is contrite and lowly in spirit, to revive the spirit of the lowly and to revive the heart of the contrite."

Isaiah 57:15

God's Words of Life on

Humility

Humble yourselves before the Lord, and he will lift you up.

James 4:10

Everyone who exalts himself will be humbled, and he who humbles himself will be exalted.

Luke 18:14

He has showed you, O man, what is good. And what does the LORD require of you? To act justly and to love mercy and to walk humbly with your God.

Micah 6:8

A man's pride brings him low, but a man of lowly spirit gains honor.

Proverbs 29:23

In his distress he sought the favor of the LORD his God and humbled himself greatly before the God of his fathers. And when he prayed to him, the LORD was moved by his entreaty and listened to his plea.

2 Chronicles 33:12–13

God's Words of Life on

Humility

Be shepherds of God's flock that is under your care, serving as overseers —not because you must, but because you are willing, as God wants you to be; not greedy for money, but eager to serve; not lording it over those entrusted to you, but being examples to the flock.

1 Peter 5:2 –3

Scripture says: "God opposes the proud but gives grace to the humble."

James 4:6

The brother in humble circumstances ought to take pride in his high position.

James 1:9

Do nothing out of selfish ambition or vain conceit, but in humility consider others better than yourselves. Each of you should look not only to your own interests, but also to the interests of others.

Philippians 2:3 –4

Be completely humble and gentle; be patient, bearing with one another in love.

Ephesians 4:2

GOD'S WORDS OF LIFE ON

HUMILITY

Let us not become conceited, provoking and envying each other.

GALATIANS 5:26

Live in harmony with one another. Do not be proud, but be willing to associate with people of low position. Do not be conceited.

ROMANS 12:16

By the grace given me I say to every one of you: Do not think of yourself more highly than you ought, but rather think of yourself with sober judgment, in accordance with the measure of faith God has given you.

ROMANS 12:3

The greatest among you should be like the youngest, and the one who rules like the one who serves. For who is greater, the one who is at the table or the one who serves? Is it not the one who is at the table? But I am among you as one who serves.

LUKE 22:26–27

God's Words of Life on

Humility

Jesus said, "Whoever welcomes this little child in my name welcomes me; and whoever welcomes me welcomes the one who sent me. For he who is least among you all —he is the greatest."

Luke 9:48

The Mighty One has done great things for me —holy is his name. His mercy extends to those who fear him, from generation to generation. He has performed mighty deeds with his arm; he has scattered those who are proud in their inmost thoughts. He has brought down rulers from their thrones but has lifted up the humble.

Luke 1:49 –52

Love is patient, love is kind. It does not envy, it does not boast, it is not proud.

1 Corinthians 13:4

The eyes of the arrogant man will be humbled and the pride of men brought low; the Lord alone will be exalted.

Isaiah 2:11

God's Words of Life on

Integrity

A Number One Necessity

If people are going to follow someone, whether into battle or in business or ministry, they want assurance that their leader can be trusted. They want to know that he or she will keep promises and follow through with commitments.

Samuel's honesty and personal integrity permeated every area of his life. These two characteristics directed how he regarded his possessions, his business dealings and his treatment of others. Samuel held himself accountable to the people he led. He opened himself up to the scrutiny of everyone. During his farewell speech, after having led Israel for decades, Samuel promised to repay anything he had unjustly taken from anyone. And the people's response: Not one person rose up to make a claim against Samuel.

People let us down again and again, because there is often a discrepancy between what they claim and what they live. The Biblical virtue of integrity points to a consistency between what is inside and what is outside, between belief and behavior, our words and our ways, our attitudes and our actions, our values and our practice. Samuel's example calls each of us to hold to this same standard of integrity. Whatever your leadership responsibilities, whether you're in charge of a multi-million-dollar business or a two-year-old child, manage your affairs with honesty. Let your personal commitment to integrity show in what you do during the day, every day. As you do so, you'll become a leader whom others will eagerly follow.

In everything set an example by doing what is good. In your teaching show integrity, seriousness and soundness of speech that cannot be condemned, so that those who oppose you may be ashamed because they have nothing bad to say about us.

TITUS 2:7–8

Give the enemy no opportunity for slander

1 TIMOTHY 5:14

The LORD detests lying lips, but he delights in men who are truthful.

PROVERBS 12:22

God's Words of Life on

Integrity

Keep the way of the Lord by doing what is right and just.

Genesis 18:19

Blessed is the man who does not condemn himself by what he approves.

Romans 14:22

The Lord abhors dishonest scales, but accurate weights are his delight.

Proverbs 11:1

To do what is right and just is more acceptable to the Lord than sacrifice.

Proverbs 21:3

Honest scales and balances are from the Lord; all the weights in the bag are of his making.

Proverbs 16:11

Shall I acquit a man with dishonest scales, with a bag of false weights?

Micah 6:11

God's Words of Life on

Integrity

Do not have two differing weights in your bag —one heavy, one light. Do not have two differing measures in your house —one large, one small. You must have accurate and honest weights and measures, so that you may live long in the land the LORD your God is giving you. For the LORD your God detests anyone who does these things, anyone who deals dishonestly.

DEUTERONOMY 25:13 –16

The priests of the temple in Jerusalem did not require an accounting from those to whom they gave the money to pay the workers, because they acted with complete honesty.

2 KINGS 12:15

The priests also gave money to the carpenters and builders to purchase dressed stone, and timber for joists and beams for the buildings that the kings of Judah had allowed to fall into ruin. The men did the work faithfully.

2 CHRONICLES 34:11

I, Nehemiah, put in charge of Jerusalem my brother Hanani, along with Hananiah the commander of the citadel, because he was a man of integrity and feared God more than most men do.

Nehemiah 7:2

The Lord detests differing weights, and dishonest scales do not please him.

Proverbs 20:23

He who walks righteously and speaks what is right, who rejects gain from extortion and keeps his hand from accepting bribes, who stops his ears against plots of murder and shuts his eyes against contemplating evil — this is the man who will dwell on the heights, whose refuge will be the mountain fortress. His bread will be supplied, and water will not fail him.

Isaiah 33:15–16

In everything, do to others what you would have them do to you, for this sums up the Law and the Prophets.

Matthew 7:12

God's Words of Life on

Integrity

You know the commandments: "Do not murder, do not commit adultery, do not steal, do not give false testimony, do not defraud, honor your father and mother."

Mark 10:19

I strive always to keep my conscience clear before God and man.

Acts 24:16

We are taking pains to do what is right, not only in the eyes of the Lord but also in the eyes of men.

2 Corinthians 8:21

Whatever is true, whatever is noble, whatever is right, whatever is pure, whatever is lovely, whatever is admirable —if anything is excellent or praiseworthy —think about such things.

Philippians 4:8

Leadership Development

A Leader's Liberation

One day a beautiful girl kissed a frog. It appeared to be just a simple kiss. As it turned out, it was not quite that simple. Regardless of what she thought, the moment she touched her soft lips to the slimy skin of the frog, a transformation occurred. The lime green frog was transformed into a handsome young prince. The prince was liberated to be all that he could be.

What that girl did for the frog, leaders do for their followers. Leaders are in a unique position to help their followers to develop their own leadership skills and to reach their full potential. They can then become all that God created them to be.

When Jesus commissioned the seventy, he knew that they would face hardship. After all, they departed without food, money or extra clothing. Yet they tasted success because they were well trained. They knew where to go and what to say. They even knew how to deal with rejection. Second, they had a clear vision: They were impelled by Jesus' urgent declaration of a plentiful harvest.

God's Words of Life on

Leadership Development

Leaders are compelled to know so many things and do so much so well. Yet nothing we can do to develop leaders is more important than mentoring. When the seventy returned they were filled with joy and shared stories of success. Not only did Jesus listen to their reports, but he praised their efforts. And, more importantly, he praised *them.* Jesus trained leaders, tested them and then rewarded them.

Listen, my sons, to a father's instruction; pay attention and gain understanding.

Proverbs 4:1

My son, keep my words and store up my commands within you. Keep my commands and you will live; guard my teachings as the apple of your eye. Bind them on your fingers; write them on the tablet of your heart.

Proverbs 7:1–3

Jesus said, "As for the person who hears my words but does not keep them, I do not judge him. For I did not come to judge the world, but to save it. There is a judge for the one who rejects me and does not accept my words; that very word which I spoke will condemn him at the last day."

John 12:47–48

Each man has his own gift from God; one has this gift, another has that.

1 Corinthians 7:7

This is a trustworthy saying. And I want you to stress these things, so that those who have trusted in God may be careful to devote themselves to doing what is good. These things are excellent and profitable for everyone.

Titus 3:8

To this you were called, because Christ suffered for you, leaving you an example, that you should follow in his steps.

1 Peter 2:21

Be imitators of God, therefore, as dearly loved children and live a life of love, just as Christ loved us and gave himself up for us as a fragrant offering and sacrifice to God.

Ephesians 5:1–2

God's Words of Life on

Leadership Development

Whoever wants to become great among you must be your servant, and whoever wants to be first must be slave of all.

Mark 10:43–44

Jesus said, "I have set you an example that you should do as I have done for you."

John 13:15

This is how we know what love is: Jesus Christ laid down his life for us. And we ought to lay down our lives for our brothers.

1 John 3:16

Dear children, let us not love with words or tongue but with actions and in truth.

1 John 3:18

In everything set them an example by doing what is good. In your teaching show integrity, seriousness and soundness of speech that cannot be condemned, so that those who oppose you may be ashamed because they have nothing bad to say about us.

Titus 2:7–8

God's Words of Life on

Leadership Development

Don't let anyone look down on you because you are young, but set an example for the believers in speech, in life, in love, in faith and in purity.

1 Timothy 4:12

Follow my example, as I follow the example of Christ.

1 Corinthians 11:1

Be shepherds of God's flock that is under your care, serving as overseers —not because you must, but because you are willing, as God wants you to be; not greedy for money, but eager to serve; not lording it over those entrusted to you, but being examples to the flock.

1 Peter 5:2–3

My son, if you accept my words and store up my commands within you . . . . then you will understand the fear of the Lord and find the knowledge of God.

Proverbs 2:1–5

God's Words of Life on

Leadership Development

Let us not love with words or tongue but with actions and in truth.

1 John 3:18

Learn to do right! Seek justice, encourage the oppressed. Defend the cause of the fatherless, plead the case of the widow.

Isaiah 1:17

This is what the Lord says: "Stand at the crossroads and look; ask for the ancient paths, ask where the good way is, and walk in it, and you will find rest for your souls."

Jeremiah 6:16

They have devoted themselves to the service of the saints. I urge you, brothers, to submit to such as these and to everyone who joins in the work, and labors at it.

1 Corinthians 16:15–16

Two are better than one, because they have a good return for their work: If one falls down, his friend can help him up. But pity the man who falls and has no one to help him up!

Ecclesiastes 4:9–10

God's Words of Life on

Leadership Qualifications

A Leadership Test

Before stepping into a leadership role, or elevating others to leadership positions, we need to do some testing to see how well we or others measure up to the qualifications God has for leaders. While the traits identified by Paul [in 1 Timothy 3] refer specifically to leaders in the church, any leader who possesses them would have the kind of leadership character of which God approves.

The summary statement for the entire list simply says, "the overseer must be above reproach" (1Tim. 3:2). Leaders in the church are to have no moral or behavioral handles that others can grab onto and say, "This disqualifies this person from leadership." A careful examination of the leader's qualifications reveals someone who has his or her private (family) and public life in balance. This person exercises moderation and humility while maintaining a good reputation with those outside the church.

One more thing. The time to discover if someone can lead isn't after they've assumed the role, but before. That's still the best policy today. While nobody perfectly measures up to the leadership qualifications in this passage, we should all strive to achieve them. With that in mind, how do you measure up? Ask God to enable you to grow in each of those areas so you can be a leader who pleases him.

The overseer must be above reproach, the husband of but one wife, temperate, self-controlled, respectable, hospitable, able to teach, not given to drunkenness, not violent but gentle, not quarrelsome, not a lover of money. He must manage his own family well and see that his children obey him with proper respect. (If anyone does not know how to manage his own family, how can he take care of God's church?) He must not be a recent convert, or he may become conceited and fall under the same judgment as the devil. He must also have a good reputation with outsiders, so that he will not fall into disgrace and into the devil's trap.

1 Timothy 3:2–7

Do your best to present yourself to God as one approved, a workman who does not need

LEADERSHIP QUALIFICATIONS

to be ashamed and who correctly handles the word of truth. Avoid godless chatter, because those who indulge in it will become more and more ungodly.

2 TIMOTHY 2:15–16

Do not merely listen to the word, and so deceive yourselves. Do what it says. Anyone who listens to the word but does not do what it says is like a man who looks at his face in a mirror and, after looking at himself, goes away and immediately forgets what he looks like. But the man who looks intently into the perfect law that gives freedom, and continues to do this, not forgetting what he has heard, but doing it—he will be blessed in what he does.

JAMES 1:22–25

The LORD said to Samuel, "Do not consider his appearance or his height, for I have rejected him. The LORD does not look at the things man looks at. Man looks at the outward appearance, but the LORD looks at the heart."

1 SAMUEL 16:7

God's Words of Life on

Obedience to God

The Cost of Obedience

According to Scripture, a fundamental factor of the quality of this life and of the next is our response to God's initiatives. Response is unavoidable; we may ignore, resist or reject God's initiatives and requirements. There may be times when obedience to God means saying no to our personal desires. When obedience to God is costly, why be obedient? All of us had better have an answer to that question before we find ourselves in the vise of a tough decision.

Many leaders have access to information or financial resources that they could use to their personal advantage. Others travel widely and almost anonymously, and have ample opportunity to compromise their purity. Still others use their position to unethically crush the competition —whether internal or external. Whether the temptation is money, sex or power, many leaders sell themselves out.

Every leader should periodically ask, "Do I have a price?" A godly leader's commitment to God should be such that he or she will obey him no matter what he or she is offered to compromise. A brief overview of Israel's history shows that the fundamental problem of God's covenant people was their repeated failure to obey God's commands. God always blessed their obedience, but their habitual disobedience was the cause of their misery and their eventual downfall.

So ask yourself, "What's my price? What would it take for me to disobey God?" Non-negotiable commitment is a crucial element in the character of a leader.

We will serve the LORD our God and obey him.

Joshua 24:24

The LORD said, "If you walk in my ways and obey my statutes and commands . . . I will give you a long life."

1 Kings 3:14

This is love: that we walk in obedience to his commands. As you have heard from the beginning, his command is that you walk in love.

2 John 6

God's Words of Life on

Obedience to God

This is how we know that we love the children of God: by loving God and carrying out his commands. This is love for God: to obey his commands. And his commands are not burdensome.

1 John 5:2–3

I have considered my ways and have turned my steps to your statutes. I will hasten and not delay to obey your commands.

Psalm 119:59–60

Those who obey his commands live in him, and he in them. And this is how we know that he lives in us: We know it by the Spirit he gave us.

1 John 3:24

All the ways of the Lord are loving and faithful for those who keep the demands of his covenant.

Psalm 25:10

I have kept my feet from every evil path so that I might obey God's word.

Psalm 119:101

God's Words of Life on

Obedience to God

From everlasting to everlasting the LORD's love is with those who fear him, and his righteousness with their children's children —with those who keep his covenant and remember to obey his precepts.

PSALM 103:17–18

We obey the Lord's commands and do what pleases him.

1 JOHN 3:22

We know that we have come to know the Lord if we obey his commands. The man who says, "I know him," but does not do what he commands is a liar, and the truth is not in him. But if anyone obeys his word, God's love is truly made complete in him.

1 JOHN 2:3–5

As obedient children, do not conform to the evil desires you had when you lived in ignorance. But just as he who called you is holy, so be holy in all you do; for it is written: "Be holy, because I am holy."

1 PETER 1:14–16

Obedience to God

Therefore, my dear friends, as you have always obeyed —not only in my presence, but now much more in my absence —continue to work out your salvation with fear and trembling, for it is God who works in you to will and to act according to his good purpose.

Philippians 2:12–13

Blessed are they who keep the Lord's statutes and seek him with all their heart. They do nothing wrong; they walk in his ways.

Psalm 119:2–3

Does the Lord delight in burnt offerings and sacrifices as much as in obeying the voice of the Lord? To obey is better than sacrifice, and to heed is better than the fat of rams.

1 Samuel 15:22

I will always obey God's law, for ever and ever.

Psalm 119:44

He who obeys instructions guards his life, but he who is contemptuous of his ways will die.

Proverbs 19:16

God's Words of Life on

Obedience to God

If our hearts do not condemn us, we have confidence before God and receive from him anything we ask, because we obey his commands and do what pleases him.

1 John 3:21–22

Circumcision is nothing and uncircumcision is nothing. Keeping God's commands is what counts.

1 Corinthians 7:19

Whoever has my commands and obeys them, he is the one who loves me. He who loves me will be loved by my Father, and I too will love him and show myself to him.

John 14:21

Jesus said, "If you love me, you will obey what I command."

John 14:15

Blessed rather are those who hear the word of God and obey it.

Luke 11:28

God's Words of Life on

Obedience to God

The LORD said, "Obey me, and I will be your God and you will be my people. Walk in all the ways I command you, that it may go well with you."

JEREMIAH 7:23

Anyone who breaks one of the least of these commandments and teaches others to do the same will be called least in the kingdom of heaven, but whoever practices and teaches these commands will be called great in the kingdom of heaven.

MATTHEW 5:19

Jesus replied, "If anyone loves me, he will obey my teaching. My Father will love him, and we will come to him and make our home with him. He who does not love me will not obey my teaching."

JOHN 14:23–24

Jesus said, "If you obey my commands, you will remain in my love, just as I have obeyed my Father's commands and remain in his love."

JOHN 15:10

GOD'S WORDS OF LIFE ON

ORGANIZATIONAL STRUCTURE

A DESIRABLE OUTCOME

Organizations are good. They gather multiple resources and focus them on a mutually desirable outcome. Well-led organizations can accomplish far more than any individual can hope to accomplish alone. Yet Scripture doesn't provide us with any rock-solid systems for organizational structure. Organizational structure is designed to channel resources to meet the task and mission of the organization. As such, it must change as resources and tasks ebb and flow.

Moses was overwhelmed by the problems of leading a large number of people. His father-in-law, Jethro, is history's first recorded management consultant. He helped Moses to see that organization and structure are essential to effective operation. Not only is work accomplished more efficiently, but also people are better served and supported in doing the work. A strong leader is approachable and willing to allow others to tweak the structure of his or her organization, if doing so will strengthen it.

The principle embodied here is that effective leaders create a structure that nurtures

Organizational Structure

the health of those they lead. Organizational structure serves rather than dominates an enterprise. Through discipline and skill we can bring greater structure and harmony into our personal and social environments. Moses did this by hand-picking potential leaders, training them and empowering them. Moses teaches us that key leaders can still maintain some control —when problems arose, he still acted as a final arbiter. But through effective delegation a leader can multiply his or her effectiveness and better meet the needs of those who require personal attention.

Everything should be done in a fitting and orderly way.

1 Corinthians 14:40

I am present with you in spirit and delight to see how orderly you are and how firm your faith in Christ is.

Colossians 2:5

Let us behave decently, as in the daytime.

Romans 13:13

GOD'S WORDS OF LIFE ON

ORGANIZATIONAL STRUCTURE

The spirits of prophets are subject to the control of prophets. For God is not a God of disorder but of peace.

1 CORINTHIANS 14:32–33

Moses took his seat to serve as judge for the people, and they stood around him from morning till evening.

When his father-in-law saw all that Moses was doing for the people, he said, "What is this you are doing for the people? Why do you alone sit as judge, while all these people stand around you from morning till evening?"

Moses answered him, "Because the people come to me to seek God's will. Whenever they have a dispute, it is brought to me, and I decide between the parties and inform them of God's decrees and laws."

Moses' father-in-law replied, "What you are doing is not good. You and these people who come to you will only wear yourselves out. The work is too heavy for you; you cannot handle it alone. Listen now to me and I will give you some advice, and may God be with you. You must be the people's representative before God and bring their disputes to him. Teach them the decrees and laws, and show them the way to live and the duties they are to perform. But select capable men from all the people —men who fear God, trustworthy men who hate dishonest gain —and appoint them as officials over thousands, hundreds, fifties and tens. Have them serve as judges for the people at all times, but have them bring every difficult case to you; the simple cases they can decide themselves. That will make your load lighter, because they will share it with you. If you do this and God so commands, you will be able to stand the strain, and all these people will go home satisfied."

Moses listened to his father-in-law and did everything he said.

Exodus 18:13 –24

Let us not be like others, who are asleep, but let us be alert and self-controlled.

1 Thessalonians 5:6

Like a city whose walls are broken down is a man who lacks self-control.

Proverbs 25:28

God's Words of Life on

Organizational Structure

Making the most of every opportunity, because the days are evil.

Ephesians 5:16

In the church God has appointed first of all apostles, second prophets, third teachers, then workers of miracles, also those having gifts of healing, those able to help others, those with gifts of administration, and those speaking in different kinds of tongues.

1 Corinthians 12:28

The Lord our God broke out in anger against us. We did not inquire of him about how to do it in the prescribed way.

1 Chronicles 15:13

I praise you for remembering me in everything and for holding to the teachings, just as I passed them on to you.

1 Corinthians 11:2

God's Words of Life on

Planning

Follow Me!

Looking ahead into the future is an integral characteristic of effective leadership. Spontaneity is valuable and sometimes necessary, but the consequences would be disastrous if most of our life's direction were left to serendipity and happenstance. Although as a leader you may not possess a crystal ball to foretell what the future will bring, you can and should be planning for what it *may* bring. Planning and evaluating performance with long-term goals and objectives in mind requires discipline, but this discipline inevitably leads to greater freedom.

Without question, God is the ultimate long-range planner. His purposes encompass the whole range from eternity to eternity and extend to every part of his dominion. From a short-range perspective, things may appear to be out of control, but God is ordering all things in such a way that they will reach a glorious consummation.

God looked far into the future and saw his glorious victory over all the forces of evil, those mighty forces that were unleashed as a result of one little bite of a piece of forbidden fruit in the Garden of Eden. Back then God unveiled a plan that would unfold thousands of years later on a cross outside of Jerusalem.

Leadership suggests movement. "Where are we heading?" is a question that every responsible leader must answer in order to have the courage to summon others to "Follow me." Take some time to discover the direction in which you and those you lead are headed.

The plans of the righteous are just, but the advice of the wicked is deceitful.

Proverbs 12:5

Job said to the Lord, "I know that you can do all things; no plan of yours can be thwarted."

Job 42:2

Surely the Sovereign Lord does nothing without revealing his plan to his servants the prophets.

Amos 3:7

God's Words of Life on

Planning

The LORD Almighty has sworn, "Surely, as I have planned, so it will be, and as I have purposed, so it will stand."

ISAIAH 14:24

Do not those who plot evil go astray? But those who plan what is good find love and faithfulness.

PROVERBS 14:22

Rescue me, O LORD, from evil men; protect me from men of violence, who devise evil plans in their hearts and stir up war every day.

PSALM 140:1–2

The plans of the diligent lead to profit as surely as haste leads to poverty.

PROVERBS 21:5

The noble man makes noble plans, and by noble deeds he stands.

ISAIAH 32:8

Make plans by seeking advice.

PROVERBS 20:18

God's Words of Life on

Planning

Do I make my plans in a worldly manner so that in the same breath I say, "Yes, yes" and "No, no"?

2 Corinthians 1:17

Plans fail for lack of counsel, but with many advisers they succeed.

Proverbs 15:22

Now listen, you who say, "Today or tomorrow we will go to this or that city, spend a year there, carry on business and make money." Why, you do not even know what will happen tomorrow. What is your life? You are a mist that appears for a little while and then vanishes. Instead, you ought to say, "If it is the Lord's will, we will live and do this or that."

James 4:13–15

The Lord foils the plans of the nations; he thwarts the purposes of the peoples. But the plans of the Lord stand firm forever, the purposes of his heart through all generations.

Psalm 33:10–11

God's Words of Life on Power & Influence

The Power to Serve

Jesus' disciples could smell it in the air. The Master had been talking about his departure, and that meant that their time to rule was imminent. While they had difficulty interpreting Jesus' words, they understood one thing clearly: As Jesus' apostles, they possessed power and authority.

Power is essential to leadership. The ability it affords an individual to influence others can be an enormous force for good. But many, like Jesus' disciples at this point in their leadership development, focus on the self-serving aspects of power. To these disciples power implied opportunity for importance. They allowed their minds to envision thrones and positions and titles. But Jesus' rebuke was stern: "None of that! Not in my kingdom."

The starting point toward responsible exercise of power is asking the fundamental question, "Why do I want it?" Many who address that question struggle with the temptation to give all the wrong answers. Some leaders expend their lives in a constant struggle to compete against and dominate others in their quest to acquire, and then defend, their positions of power. But Jesus implied that there is only one correct answer to this question: "I want power and influence because with it I can better serve God, people and this organization." As a leader, think about ways in which you can use your power in an exalted and benevolent way. Anything less than that response violates God's trust in you as one who has been granted power.

Jesus looked at them and said, "With man this is impossible, but with God all things are possible."

Matthew 19:26

I am the Lord, the God of all mankind. Is anything too hard for me?

Jeremiah 32:27

The Lord is slow to anger and great in power; the Lord will not leave the guilty unpunished. His way is in the whirlwind and the storm, and clouds are the dust of his feet.

Nahum 1:3

God's Words of Life on

Power & Influence

The LORD said, "See now that I myself am He! There is no god besides me. I put to death and I bring to life, I have wounded and I will heal, and no one can deliver out of my hand."

DEUTERONOMY 32:39

All the peoples of the earth are regarded as nothing. God does as he pleases with the powers of heaven and the peoples of the earth. No one can hold back his hand or say to him: "What have you done?"

DANIEL 4:35

Wealth and honor come from you, O LORD; you are the ruler of all things. In your hands are strength and power to exalt and give strength to all. Now, our God, we give you thanks, and praise your glorious name.

1 CHRONICLES 29:12–13

You are awesome, O God, in your sanctuary; the God of Israel gives power and strength to his people. Praise be to God!

PSALM 68:35

God's Words of Life on

Power & Influence

Your strength will equal your days.

Deuteronomy 33:25

The Lord gives strength to his people; the Lord blesses his people with peace.

Psalm 29:11

"I will strengthen them in the Lord and in his name they will walk," declares the Lord.

Zechariah 10:12

I can do everything through God who gives me strength.

Philippians 4:13

Being strengthened with all power according to the Lord's glorious might so that you may have great endurance and patience.

Colossians 1:11

These are but the outer fringe of God's works; how faint the whisper we hear of him! Who then can understand the thunder of his power?

Job 26:14

God's Words of Life on

Power & Influence

God has made everything beautiful in its time. He has also set eternity in the hearts of men; yet they cannot fathom what God has done from beginning to end.

Ecclesiastes 3:11

God's wisdom is profound, his power is vast. Who has resisted him and come out unscathed?

Job 9:4

Your arm is endued with power, O Lord; your hand is strong, your right hand exalted.

Psalm 89:13

Your right hand, O Lord, was majestic in power. Your right hand, O Lord, shattered the enemy.

Exodus 15:6

Be strong in the Lord and in his mighty power.

Ephesians 6:10

GOD'S WORDS OF LIFE ON

POWER & INFLUENCE

Yours, O LORD, is the greatness and the power and the glory and the majesty and the splendor, for everything in heaven and earth is yours. Yours, O LORD, is the kingdom; you are exalted as head over all. Wealth and honor come from you; you are the ruler of all things. In your hands are strength and power to exalt and give strength to all.

1 CHRONICLES 29:11–12

I pray that out of his glorious riches God may strengthen you with power through his Spirit in your inner being, so that Christ may dwell in your hearts through faith. And I pray that you, being rooted and established in love, may have power, together with all the saints, to grasp how wide and long and high and deep is the love of Christ.

EPHESIANS 3:16–18

As for me, I am filled with power, with the Spirit of the LORD, and with justice and might.

MICAH 3:8

Priorities

The Demands of Priorities

Life gets confusing and conflicting. We have to decide what matters most or we become victims of the loudest or latest demands. No leader will ever lack for things to occupy his or her time and energy. Because that's the case, every leader must answer an important question: "What should be my priorities?"

Jesus told the story of a man whose main priority was himself and his possessions. The man wanted to accumulate wealth to secure his own future. Now, any retirement investment consultant will tell you that saving for the future is a good pursuit. But the rich fool started with the wrong motives. Unfortunately he died before he could either expand his business or enjoy retirement. Jesus applied this parable to anybody whose priorities reveal a heart absorbed with self instead of God.

Effective leaders have the ability to discern not only the difference between the good and the bad, but also the difference between the good and the best. Since we cannot do everything well, we must carefully choose a few things on which we will concentrate. Ultimately, our purpose for living should be to bring honor to God rather than to bring pleasure to ourselves. With that purpose in mind we can set our priorities by discovering what will bring the greatest recognition to God. If we do that, unlike the fool in the parable, we'll be rich in God's eyes.

I was not disobedient to the vision from heaven.

ACTS 26:19

We do not want you to become lazy, but to imitate those who through faith and patience inherit what has been promised.

HEBREWS 6:12

Since we are surrounded by such a great cloud of witnesses, let us throw off everything that hinders and the sin that so easily entangles, and let us run with perseverance the race marked out for us. Let us fix our eyes on Jesus, the author and perfecter of our faith, who for the joy set before him endured the cross, scorning its shame, and sat down at the right hand of the throne of God.

HEBREWS 12:1–2

Priorities

If your eye causes you to sin, pluck it out. It is better for you to enter the kingdom of God with one eye than to have two eyes and be thrown into hell.

Mark 9:47

Jesus said, "This, then, is how you should pray: 'Our Father in heaven, hallowed be your name, your kingdom come, your will be done on earth as it is in heaven.'"

Matthew 6:9–10

By faith Moses, when he had grown up, refused to be known as the son of Pharaoh's daughter. He chose to be mistreated along with the people of God rather than to enjoy the pleasures of sin for a short time. He regarded disgrace for the sake of Christ as of greater value than the treasures of Egypt, because he was looking ahead to his reward.

Hebrews 11:24–26

Honor men like him, because he almost died for the work of Christ, risking his life to make up for the help you could not give me.

Philippians 2:29–30

God's Words of Life on

Priorities

Whatever was to my profit I now consider loss for the sake of Christ.

Philippians 3:7

Whatever happens, conduct yourselves in a manner worthy of the gospel of Christ.

Philippians 1:27

Make my joy complete by being like-minded, having the same love, being one in spirit and purpose. Do nothing out of selfish ambition or vain conceit, but in humility consider others better than yourselves. Each of you should look not only to your own interests, but also to the interests of others. Your attitude should be the same as that of Christ Jesus.

Philippians 2:2–5

Do not be foolish, but understand what the Lord's will is.

Ephesians 5:17

Let us not love with words or tongue but with actions and in truth.

1 John 3:18

God's Words of Life on

Priorities

May the God of peace, who through the blood of the eternal covenant brought back from the dead our Lord Jesus, that great Shepherd of the sheep, equip you with everything good for doing his will, and may he work in us what is pleasing to him, through Jesus Christ, to whom be glory for ever and ever. Amen.

Hebrews 13:20 –21

I consider my life worth nothing to me, if only I may finish the race and complete the task the Lord Jesus has given me —the task of testifying to the gospel of God's grace.

Acts 20:24

Without faith it is impossible to please God, because anyone who comes to him must believe that he exists and that he rewards those who earnestly seek him.

Hebrews 11:6

How great is your goodness, which you have stored up for those who fear you, which you bestow in the sight of men on those who take refuge in you.

Psalm 31:19

Purpose

A Passion for God

Paul accomplished an astounding amount in two decades of ministry. What drove him to carry out the work that he did? Effective leaders, like Paul, are those who have figured out what they stand for. They have identified their purpose and pursue it with a passion.

Before his dramatic conversion, Paul followed a different purpose in life. As a member of the Pharisees, Paul had attained the highest levels of stature. He could have boasted about his religious training, heritage and practice. His credentials would have impressed the most devoted Jew. Yet Paul considered all he had attained through religious effort to be garbage when compared with the value of knowing Christ. Paul was more than happy to throw away all he had attained in order to know Christ.

Paul preached that in Christ he and all believers possess all the righteousness of God. And because of the infinite worth of knowing Christ, Paul devoted his life to knowing the Savior. That was his purpose and his passion.

Purpose

And that purpose shaped all he did and influenced all he led.

It is ironic that people tend to put more effort into planning a two-week vacation than they do in thinking about the destiny of their earthly journey. Few people can articulate a clear purpose statement for their lives. As godly leaders, our purpose in life needs to be directed toward God and his kingdom.

Why do you get out of bed in the morning? What is your life purpose?

Though we live in the world, we do not wage war as the world does. The weapons we fight with are not the weapons of the world. On the contrary, they have divine power to demolish strongholds. We demolish arguments and every pretension that sets itself up against the knowledge of God, and we take captive every thought to make it obedient to Christ.

2 Corinthians 10:3–5

My soul clings to you; your right hand upholds me.

Psalm 63:8

GOD'S WORDS OF LIFE ON

PURPOSE

I consider everything a loss compared to the surpassing greatness of knowing Christ Jesus my Lord, for whose sake I have lost all things. I consider them rubbish, that I may gain Christ and be found in him, not having a righteousness of my own that comes from the law, but that which is through faith in Christ —the righteousness that comes from God and is by faith. I want to know Christ and the power of his resurrection and the fellowship of sharing in his sufferings, becoming like him in his death, and so, somehow, to attain to the resurrection from the dead. Not that I have already obtained all this, or have already been made perfect, but I press on to take hold of that for which Christ Jesus took hold of me.

PHILIPPIANS 3:8–12

"The eyes of the Lord are on the righteous and his ears are attentive to their prayer, but the face of the Lord is against those who do evil." Who is going to harm you if you are eager to do good? But even if you should suffer for what is right, you are blessed.

1 PETER 3:12–14

God's Words of Life on

Purpose

See to it that no one misses the grace of God and that no bitter root grows up to cause trouble and defile many.

Hebrews 12:15

Pursue righteousness, godliness, faith, love, endurance and gentleness. Fight the good fight of the faith. Take hold of the eternal life to which you were called.

1 Timothy 6:11–12

I have fought the good fight, I have finished the race, I have kept the faith. Now there is in store for me the crown of righteousness, which the Lord, the righteous Judge, will award to me on that day—and not only to me, but also to all who have longed for his appearing.

2 Timothy 4:7–8

Fight the good fight, holding on to faith and a good conscience. Some have rejected these and so have shipwrecked their faith.

1 Timothy 1:18–19

Reconciled Relationships

The Bible is all about relationships. God is a personal being who has paid a great price to make it possible for us to enter a relationship with him through the merits of Jesus Christ. He wants this relationship, in turn, to be made visible in our relationships with others.

Sometimes strengthening relationships requires both the grace of God and a deep reservoir of love. That was certainly the case with Hosea. As a prophet to Israel, Hosea's job was to predict the nation's exile and later restoration. In order to illustrate God's love for the nation, he was commanded to marry Gomer, a prostitute. Hosea did so, but his heart was broken when she proved unfaithful and eventually left him. Later, Hosea forgave her and renewed their marriage relationship.

Hosea's love for Gomer serves as a picture of God's love for his unfaithful people. And it serves as an example for us to follow. Savvy leaders understand that the better their relationships with followers, the more effective their leadership. At times, every leader is called upon by God to seek out, forgive and restore those who have wronged him or her. Such actions do indeed require both the grace and love of God. When God calls on you to seek reconciliation with someone who has hurt you, how will you respond? Remember, great leaders are well acquainted with forgiveness.

Bear with each other and forgive whatever grievances you may have against one another. Forgive as the Lord forgave you.

Colossians 3:13

Do not be yoked together with unbelievers. For what do righteousness and wickedness have in common? Or what fellowship can light have with darkness?. . . . What does a believer have in common with an unbeliever?. . . . For we are the temple of the living God. As God has said: "I will live with them and walk among them, and I will be their God, and they will be my people." "Therefore come out from them and be separate," says the Lord.

2 Corinthians 6:14 –17

God's Words of Life on Relationships

For by the grace given me I say to every one of you: Do not think of yourself more highly than you ought, but rather think of yourself with sober judgment, in accordance with the measure of faith God has given you. Just as each of us has one body with many members, and these members do not all have the same function, so in Christ we who are many form one body, and each member belongs to all the others.

Romans 12:3–5

Two are better than one, because they have a good return for their work: If one falls down, his friend can help him up. But pity the man who falls and has no one to help him up! Though one may be overpowered, two can defend themselves. A cord of three strands is not quickly broken.

Ecclesiastes 4:9–12

In everything set them an example by doing what is good. In your teaching show integrity, seriousness and soundness of speech that cannot be condemned, so that those who oppose you may be ashamed because they have nothing bad to say about us.

Titus 2:7–8

God's Words of Life on

Relationships

As iron sharpens iron, so one man sharpens another.

Proverbs 27:17

Be completely humble and gentle; be patient, bearing with one another in love. Make every effort to keep the unity of the Spirit through the bond of peace.

Ephesians 4:2–3

Then Peter began to speak: "I now realize how true it is that God does not show favoritism but accepts men from every nation who fear him and do what is right."

Acts 10:34–35

My brothers, as believers in our glorious Lord Jesus Christ, don't show favoritism.

James 2:1

See that you do not look down on one of these little ones. For I tell you that their angels in heaven always see the face of my Father in heaven.

Matthew 18:10

God's Words of Life on
Relationships

The Lord does not look at the things man looks at. Man looks at the outward appearance, but the Lord looks at the heart.

1 Samuel 16:7

Do not rebuke an older man harshly, but exhort him as if he were your father. Treat younger men as brothers, older women as mothers, and younger women as sisters, with absolute purity.

1 Timothy 5:1–2

Carry each other's burdens, and in this way you will fulfill the law of Christ.

Galatians 6:2

Give everyone what you owe him: If you owe taxes, pay taxes; if revenue, then revenue; if respect, then respect; if honor, then honor. Let no debt remain outstanding, except the continuing debt to love one another.

Romans 13:7–8

Peacemakers who sow in peace raise a harvest of righteousness.

James 3:18

God's Words of Life on

Rewards

A Merited Motivation

There's no getting around it: People are motivated by rewards. God certainly understands this. Many people perceive God as a cosmic Scrooge who enjoys making people squirm and reluctantly dispenses rewards for good behavior. But the Biblical portrait of God in both Testaments is quite the opposite. The Scriptures consistently present God as the lover of our souls who delights in rewarding us with his joy. The Bible is filled with promises of the rewards God will give to those who follow him.

Perhaps no chapter in the Bible illustrates this better than Hebrews 11. A careful reading of this chapter reveals that many of these great men and women exercised their faith but were able only to *look forward to* their reward; they never fully realized that reward during their lifetime. Indeed, some even endured hardship in anticipation of the promised reward. Abraham, Noah, Enoch, Jacob, Joseph and Moses all lived a life of faith in spite of the fact that their reward was in the "distance."

God's Words of Life on

Rewards

Most of us would quickly become bored with our work if there were no rewards beyond the money. Effective leaders understand the human need for reward, and they make use of recognition and compensation to lift morale and improve performance. A reward can be as simple and effective as regular encouragement or as extensive and long-range as a profit sharing program. Without a motivational system, workers will likely be inclined to get by with minimum levels of effort and performance.

Do not let this Book of the Law depart from your mouth; meditate on it day and night, so that you may be careful to do everything written in it. Then you will be prosperous and successful.

Joshua 1:8

This is what the Lord says —your Redeemer, the Holy One of Israel: "I am the Lord your God, who teaches you what is best for you, who directs you in the way you should go."

Isaiah 48:17

God's Words of Life on

Rewards

I pray that you may enjoy good health and that all may go well with you, even as your soul is getting along well.

3 John 12

Remember the Lord your God, for it is he who gives you the ability to produce wealth, and so confirms his covenant.

Deuteronomy 8:18

His delight is in the law of the Lord, and on his law he meditates day and night. He is like a tree planted by streams of water, which yields its fruit in season and whose leaf does not wither. Whatever he does prospers.

Psalm 1:2–3

You will have success if you are careful to observe the decrees and laws that the Lord gave Moses for Israel. Be strong and courageous. Do not be afraid or discouraged.

1 Chronicles 22:13

Commit to the Lord whatever you do, and your plans will succeed.

Proverbs 16:3

Rewards

Let love and faithfulness never leave you; bind them around your neck, write them on the tablet of your heart. Then you will win favor and a good name in the sight of God and man.

PROVERBS 3:3–4

If they obey and serve him, they will spend the rest of their days in prosperity and their years in contentment.

JOB 36:11

"If your enemy is hungry, feed him; if he is thirsty, give him something to drink. In doing this, you will heap burning coals on his head." Do not be overcome by evil, but overcome evil with good.

ROMANS 12:20–21

Delight yourself in the LORD and he will give you the desires of your heart. Commit your way to the LORD; trust in him and he will do this: He will make your righteousness shine like the dawn, the justice of your cause like the noonday sun.

PSALM 37:4–6

God's Words of Life on

Rewards

Honor the LORD with your wealth, with the firstfruits of all your crops; then your barns will be filled to overflowing, and your vats will brim over with new wine.

PROVERBS 3:9–10

The LORD will open the heavens, the storehouse of his bounty, to send rain on your land in season and to bless all the work of your hands. You will lend to many nations but will borrow from none. The LORD will make you the head, not the tail. If you pay attention to the commands of the LORD your God that I give you this day and carefully follow them, you will always be at the top, never at the bottom.

DEUTERONOMY 28:12–13

By wisdom a house is built, and through understanding it is established.

PROVERBS 24:3

From the fruit of his lips a man is filled with good things as surely as the work of his hands rewards him.

PROVERBS 12:14

GOD'S WORDS OF LIFE ON

REWARDS

Make it your ambition to lead a quiet life, to mind your own business and to work with your hands, just as we told you, so that your daily life may win the respect of outsiders and so that you will not be dependent on anybody.

1 THESSALONIANS 4:11–12

Do not forget to do good and to share with others, for with such sacrifices God is pleased.

HEBREWS 13:16

The LORD rewards every man for his righteousness and faithfulness.

1 SAMUEL 26:23

Without faith it is impossible to please God, because anyone who comes to him must believe that he exists and that he rewards those who earnestly seek him.

HEBREWS 11:6

God's Words of Life on

Risk Taking

No Risks with God

Leaders need courage to make tough decisions. Joshua certainly faced such a crisis in his leadership role. Not only did he have to contend with the military powers rooted in the promised land, but he also had to face them with an untrained band of nomadic shepherds.

God realized Joshua's need for courage and gave him guidance that would strengthen his faith. First, he reminded Joshua of his faithfulness to keep all of his promises. Joshua's success didn't rest on a military strategy or well-trained army, but on the faithfulness of God. Second, God commanded Joshua to meditate on his words. The "Book of the Law" would give the wisdom and encouragement Joshua would need to courageously lead the nation. Third, God promised to be personally present with Joshua. No matter how intimidating the enemy or how rebellious the people, God would always be at his side.

The same sources of courage that empowered Joshua are available today for any leader who will accept them. When faced with a risky business decision, the godly leader will look to God in prayer and to God's revealed Word for the perspective and courage needed to make the right choice.

Leadership, by its very nature, inspires people to move in directions they would not otherwise have been willing to take. From time to time, good leadership requires excursions into unexplored territory, and draws on a leader's courage. Let God's words to Joshua supply you with the courage you need.

"For my thoughts are not your thoughts, neither are your ways my ways," declares the LORD. "As the heavens are higher than the earth, so are my ways higher than your ways and my thoughts than your thoughts."

ISAIAH 55:8–9

Call to me and I will answer you and tell you great and unsearchable things you do not know.

JEREMIAH 33:3

If God is for us, who can be against us?

ROMANS 8:31

God's Words of Life on

Risk Taking

God is faithful; he will not let you be tempted beyond what you can bear. But when you are tempted, he will also provide a way out so that you can stand up under it.

1 Corinthians 10:13

A righteous man may have many troubles, but the Lord delivers him from them all.

Psalm 34:19

Let us hold unswervingly to the hope we profess, for he who promised is faithful.

Hebrews 10:23

Let us acknowledge the Lord; let us press on to acknowledge him. As surely as the sun rises, he will appear; he will come to us like the winter rains, like the spring rains that water the earth.

Hosea 6:3

We know that in all things God works for the good of those who love him, who have been called according to his purpose.

Romans 8:28

God's Words of Life on

Risk Taking

So do not fear, for I am with you; do not be dismayed, for I am your God. I will strengthen you and help you; I will uphold you with my righteous right hand.

Isaiah 41:10

I will make an everlasting covenant with them: I will never stop doing good to them, and I will inspire them to fear me, so that they will never turn away from me.

Jeremiah 32:40

Your love, O Lord, endures forever —do not abandon the works of your hands.

Psalm 138:8

When you ask, you do not receive, because you ask with wrong motives, that you may spend what you get on your pleasures.

James 4:3

Be strong and courageous. Do not be terrified; do not be discouraged, for the Lord your God will be with you wherever you go.

Joshua 1:9

GOD'S WORDS OF LIFE ON

RISK TAKING

When Jesus looked up and saw a great crowd coming toward him, he said to Philip, "Where shall we buy bread for these people to eat?" He asked this only to test him, for he already had in mind what he was going to do. Philip answered him, "Eight months' wages would not buy enough bread for each one to have a bite!" Another of his disciples, Andrew, Simon Peter's brother, spoke up, "Here is a boy with five small barley loaves and two small fish, but how far will they go among so many?" Jesus said, "Have the people sit down." There was plenty of grass in that place, and the men sat down, about five thousand of them. Jesus then took the loaves, gave thanks, and distributed to those who were seated as much as they wanted.

JOHN 6:5 –11

All a man's ways seem right to him, but the LORD weighs the heart.

PROVERBS 21:2

Cast your cares on the LORD and he will sustain you; he will never let the righteous fall.

PSALM 55:22

God's Words of Life on

Risk Taking

The lowly he sets on high, and those who mourn are lifted to safety. He thwarts the plans of the crafty, so that their hands achieve no success.

Job 5:11–12

Have I not commanded you? Be strong and courageous. Do not be terrified; do not be discouraged, for the Lord your God will be with you wherever you go.

Joshua 1:9

Commit your way to the Lord; trust in him and he will do this: He will make your righteousness shine like the dawn, the justice of your cause like the noonday sun.

Psalm 37:5–6

Blessed is the man who trusts in the Lord, whose confidence is in him. He will be like a tree planted by the water that sends out its roots by the stream. It does not fear when heat comes; its leaves are always green. It has no worries in a year of drought and never fails to bear fruit.

Jeremiah 17:7–8

God's Words of Life on Self-Discipline

Doing What Needs to Be Done

Self-discipline may be defined simply as that quality that allows a person to do what needs to be done when he or she doesn't feel like doing it. Composure, presence of mind, coolheadedness, patience, self-possession, restraint —only a few people display these qualities, and those who do usually make effective leaders.

The apostle Paul understood the importance of discipline. As followers of Christ our spiritual lives form the core of our character. We're to be like runners. During the course of a race, runners don't stagger from one lane to another. They rivet their attention on the finish line and run a disciplined race toward it.

Paul trained for his daily spiritual journey like a world-class athlete because he wanted to have the self-control to finish the race without being disqualified. Godly leaders need to cultivate this same kind of spiritual fitness. Doing so can and will affect other areas of leadership life —how we treat others, where we go for answers to major decisions, and the skills we use in accomplishing our daily tasks.

If you want to be an effective leader, identify the habits you need to build into your life so you can lead with diligence —habits such as physical fitness, balance between work and home, financial and personal accountability, and the like. Strap on your shoes and get going. Disciplined habits will give you the momentum you need to not only move forward, but also to run your earthly race with strength and purpose.

Love the Lord your God with all your heart and with all your soul and with all your strength.

Deuteronomy 6:5

Be very careful to keep the commandment and the law that Moses the servant of the Lord gave you: to love the Lord your God, to walk in all his ways, to obey his commands, to hold fast to him and to serve him with all your heart and all your soul.

Joshua 22:5

God's Words of Life on

Self-Discipline

O Lord, God of Israel, there is no God like you in heaven above or on earth below—you who keep your covenant of love with your servants who continue wholeheartedly in your way.

1 Kings 8:23

Surely you desire truth in the inner parts; you teach me wisdom in the inmost place.

Psalm 51:6

You will keep in perfect peace him whose mind is steadfast, because he trusts in you.

Isaiah 26:3

The mind of sinful man is death, but the mind controlled by the Spirit is life and peace.

Romans 8:6

The kingdom of God is not a matter of eating and drinking, but of righteousness, peace and joy in the Holy Spirit.

Romans 14:17

Blessed are those who hunger and thirst for righteousness, for they will be filled.

Matthew 5:6

God's Words of Life on

Self-Discipline

Since, then, you have been raised with Christ, set your hearts on things above, where Christ is seated at the right hand of God. Set your minds on things above, not on earthly things.

Colossians 3:1–2

Do not work for food that spoils, but for food that endures to eternal life, which the Son of Man will give you. On him God the Father has placed his seal of approval.

John 6:27

Jesus said, "I will ask the Father, and he will give you another Counselor to be with you forever—the Spirit of truth. The world cannot accept him, because it neither sees him nor knows him. But you know him, for he lives with you and will be in you."

John 14:16–17

The righteous requirements of the law might be fully met in us, who do not live according to the sinful nature but according to the Spirit.

Romans 8:4

God's Words of Life on

Self-Discipline

Only be careful, and watch yourselves closely so that you do not forget the things your eyes have seen or let them slip from your heart as long as you live. Teach them to your children and to their children after them.

Deuteronomy 4:9

Be careful that you do not forget the Lord your God, failing to observe his commands, his laws and his decrees that I am giving you this day. Otherwise, when you eat and are satisfied, when you build fine houses and settle down, and when your herds and flocks grow large and your silver and gold increase and all you have is multiplied, then your heart will become proud and you will forget the Lord your God.

Deuteronomy 8:11–14

If we had forgotten the name of our God or spread out our hands to a foreign god, would not God have discovered it, since he knows the secrets of the heart?

Psalm 44:20–21

This is what the Lord says: "Stand at the crossroads and look; ask for the ancient paths,

Self-Discipline

ask where the good way is, and walk in it, and you will find rest for your souls."

Jeremiah 6:16

Then those who feared the Lord talked with each other, and the Lord listened and heard. A scroll of remembrance was written in his presence concerning those who feared the Lord and honored his name. "They will be mine," says the Lord Almighty, "in the day when I make up my treasured possession. I will spare them, just as in compassion a man spares his son who serves him."

Malachi 3:16–17

Grow in the grace and knowledge of our Lord and Savior Jesus Christ. To him be glory both now and forever! Amen.

2 Peter 3:18

Do your best to present yourself to God as one approved, a workman who does not need to be ashamed and who correctly handles the word of truth.

2 Timothy 2:15

Lead by Serving

A leader can select from two fundamental but opposing orientations toward his or her organization. One paradigm prompts him or her to *take from* the organization as many perks and privileges as possible. In this model, the organization exists to provide a title, a job, status and service. The second orientation asks the leader to evaluate what he or she can contribute or *put into* the organization. In this scenario the leader takes what is needed from the organization, but his or her passion is to make it great, to serve its needs. The leader following the latter course is a servant leader, and Barnabas effectively modeled this approach. His life teaches its systemic principle. Simply put, Barnabas was a man who was convinced that God had placed him on earth to help others to live productive and satisfying lives.

The manner in which a leader uses his or her power will indicate the quality of his or her leadership. Good leaders do good things. Their lives matter. That's good. Servant leaders do great things. They help others' lives to matter by serving them. Servant leadership is great leadership. Barnabas's life illustrates numerous leadership truths, but servant leadership is certainly one of the most important. Paul singled out Timothy as one of a rare breed when he commended him to the Philippian church as a leader who would serve them well. Our power is to be used to serve others.

The greatest among you will be your servant.

MATTHEW 23:11

Whoever wants to become great among you must be your servant, and whoever wants to be first must be slave of all.

MARK 10:43–44

Jesus told his disciples, "The greatest among you should be like the youngest, and the one who rules like the one who serves. For who is greater, the one who is at the table or the one who serves? Is it not the one who is at the table? But I am among you as one who serves."

LUKE 22:26–27

God's Words of Life on

Servant Leadership

Jesus said, "I have set you an example that you should do as I have done for you. I tell you the truth, no servant is greater than his master, nor is a messenger greater than the one who sent him."

John 13:15–16

Though I am free and belong to no man, I make myself a slave to everyone, to win as many as possible. To the Jews I became like a Jew, to win the Jews. To those under the law I became like one under the law (though I myself am not under the law), so as to win those under the law. To those not having the law I became like one not having the law (though I am not free from God's law but am under Christ's law), so as to win those not having the law. To the weak I became weak, to win the weak. I have become all things to all men so that by all possible means I might save some.

1 Corinthians 9:19–22

There are different kinds of service, but the same Lord.

1 Corinthians 12:5

God's Words of Life on Servant Leadership

Your attitude should be the same as that of Christ Jesus: Who, being in very nature God, did not consider equality with God something to be grasped, but made himself nothing, taking the very nature of a servant, being made in human likeness. And being found in appearance as a man, he humbled himself and became obedient to death —even death on a cross!

Philippians 2:5 –8

Be very careful to keep the commandment and the law that Moses the servant of the Lord gave you: to love the Lord your God, to walk in all his ways, to obey his commands, to hold fast to him and to serve him with all your heart and all your soul.

Joshua 22:5

Whoever wants to save his life will lose it, but whoever loses his life for me will find it.

Matthew 16:25

It is the Lord your God you must follow, and him you must revere. Keep his commands and obey him; serve him and hold fast to him.

Deuteronomy 13:4

God's Words of Life on

Servant Leadership

Jesus said to him, "Away from me, Satan! For it is written: 'Worship the Lord your God, and serve him only.'"

Matthew 4:10

If serving the Lord seems undesirable to you, then choose for yourselves this day whom you will serve . . . . as for me and my household, we will serve the Lord.

Joshua 24:15

Be devoted to one another in brotherly love. Honor one another above yourselves. Never be lacking in zeal, but keep your spiritual fervor, serving the Lord.

Romans 12:10–11

What does the Lord your God ask of you but to fear the Lord your God, to walk in all his ways, to love him, to serve the Lord your God with all your heart and with all your soul, and to observe the Lord's commands and decrees that I am giving you today for your own good?

Deuteronomy 10:12–13

God's Words of Life on
Servant Leadership

Be sure to fear the LORD and serve him faithfully with all your heart; consider what great things he has done for you.

1 Samuel 12:24

Whoever wants to become great among you must be your servant, and whoever wants to be first must be your slave.

Matthew 20:26–27

Jesus said, "Whoever welcomes this little child in my name welcomes me; and whoever welcomes me welcomes the one who sent me. For he who is least among you all—he is the greatest."

Luke 9:48

If anyone speaks, he should do it as one speaking the very words of God. If anyone serves, he should do it with the strength God provides, so that in all things God may be praised through Jesus Christ. To him be the glory and the power for ever and ever. Amen.

1 Peter 4:11

Situational Leadership

Leadership As Needed

Jesus chose twelve men and developed them into the church's first leaders. Within a few short years he would delegate the continuance of his kingdom work to them.

Even a casual study of the manner in which Jesus prepared the twelve apostles shows us how effectively he adapted his leadership activity to the realities of the situation. He instructed them when they were uninformed, directed them when they were confused, prodded them when they were reluctant and encouraged them when they were downhearted. When they were ready, he allotted them limited tasks and responsibilities and then participated with them, guiding them through their assignments. Finally, he empowered and commissioned them as his apostles.

The Master Teacher shows us that effective leadership is situational. The leader's whim or desire (even when that leader is Jesus) is not what drives intelligent action. Effectiveness in leadership is driven by what the followers need. Jesus observed and understood what his followers needed, and he supplied it. He always interacted with them within the situation and responded appropriately to it. And within three years these obscure Galileans began to change the world.

As we observe Jesus' training of the twelve in the Gospels, we notice how consistently his actions were exactly appropriate to the situation. Jesus was very intentional about situational leadership. Leaders who can analyze a situation and adapt their leadership activity to address it can function as servant leaders and as transformational leaders, and they can profoundly affect the lives of their followers.

In your unfailing love you will lead the people you have redeemed. In your strength you will guide them to your holy dwelling.

Exodus 15:13

You are my lamp, O Lord; the Lord turns my darkness into light.

2 Samuel 22:29

Lead me, O Lord, in your righteousness because of my enemies —make straight your way before me.

Psalm 5:8

God's Words of Life on

Situational Leadership

He makes me lie down in green pastures, he leads me beside quiet waters, he restores my soul. He guides me in paths of righteousness for his name's sake.

Psalm 23:2–3

Show me your ways, O Lord, teach me your paths; guide me in your truth and teach me, for you are God my Savior, and my hope is in you all day long.

Psalm 25:4–5

For this God is our God for ever and ever; he will be our guide even to the end.

Psalm 48:14

You guide me with your counsel, and afterward you will take me into glory.

Psalm 73:24

Let the morning bring me word of your unfailing love, for I have put my trust in you. Show me the way I should go, for to you I lift up my soul.

Psalm 143:8

Situational Leadership

See if there is any offensive way in me, and lead me in the way everlasting.

Psalm 139:24

I walk in the way of righteousness, along the paths of justice.

Proverbs 8:20

Blessed are they whose ways are blameless, who walk according to the law of the Lord.

Psalm 119:1

Teach me to do your will, for you are my God; may your good Spirit lead me on level ground.

Psalm 143:10

Keep your servant also from willful sins; may they not rule over me. Then will I be blameless, innocent of great transgression. May the words of my mouth and the meditation of my heart be pleasing in your sight, O Lord, my Rock and my Redeemer.

Psalm 19:13–14

God's Words of Life on

Situational Leadership

Test me, O Lord, and try me, examine my heart and my mind; for your love is ever before me, and I walk continually in your truth.

Psalm 26:2–3

Since you are my rock and my fortress, for the sake of your name lead and guide me.

Psalm 31:3

I the Lord search the heart and examine the mind, to reward a man according to his conduct, according to what his deeds deserve.

Jeremiah 17:10

If you are pleased with me, teach me your ways so I may know you and continue to find favor with you.

Exodus 33:13

Teach me, and I will be quiet; show me where I have been wrong.

Job 6:24

Teach me your way, O Lord; lead me in a straight path because of my oppressors.

Psalm 27:11

God's Words of Life on

Situational Leadership

Surely you desire truth in the inner parts; you teach me wisdom in the inmost place.

Psalm 51:6

Let me understand the teaching of your precepts; then I will meditate on your wonders.

Psalm 119:27

Teach me, O Lord, to follow your decrees; then I will keep them to the end. Give me understanding, and I will keep your law and obey it with all my heart. Direct me in the path of your commands, for there I find delight. Turn my heart toward your statutes and not toward selfish gain. Turn my eyes away from worthless things; preserve my life according to your word.

Psalm 119:33–37

Show me, O Lord, my life's end and the number of my days; let me know how fleeting is my life. You have made my days a mere handbreadth; the span of my years is as nothing before you. Each man's life is but a breath.

Psalm 39:4–5

GOD'S WORDS OF LIFE ON

SITUATIONAL LEADERSHIP

May the Lord direct your hearts into God's love and Christ's perseverance.

1 THESSALONIANS 3:5

Good and upright is the LORD; therefore he instructs sinners in his ways. He guides the humble in what is right and teaches them his way.

PSALM 25:8–9

Teach me your way, O LORD, and I will walk in your truth; give me an undivided heart, that I may fear your name.

PSALM 86:11

The LORD will guide you always; he will satisfy your needs in a sun-scorched land and will strengthen your frame. You will be like a well-watered garden, like a spring whose waters never fail.

ISAIAH 58:11

God's Words of Life on Stewardship

Faithful Investments

Consider for a moment that everyone on earth has the same amount of time in every day. President or paper boy, housewife or executive, farmer or financier —they all have exactly twenty-four hours in each day.

What differentiates people isn't the amount of time available to them but the manner in which they exercise their gifts and talents within the available time. That's what stewardship is about: faithfully developing and using our gifts, talents and resources within the amount of time God has allotted to us.

Within every stewardship relationship there are two parties involved: the master who hands out the resources and will one day ask for an accounting; and the steward who is entrusted with the resources and must eventually answer for how they were invested.

When Jesus taught about his second coming, he drove home one important lesson: Only faithful stewards will be prepared for his return. The parable he used to make this point involved three servants who each received a sum of money from his master before that master departed on a long journey. Upon his return the master discovered that two of the servants had invested the money and that one had buried it.

When the servant who had buried the money began offering excuses, the master refused to accept them. Instead, he rebuked the lazy servant and punished him severely.

Leaders are stewards. They manage multiple resources because they direct others in using *their* own resources. Consider ways of investing the multiple resources God has placed under your trust.

Turn my heart toward your statutes and not toward selfish gain.

Psalm 119:36

The Lord is my shepherd, I shall not be in want.

Psalm 23:1

No one can serve two masters. Either he will hate the one and love the other, or he will be devoted to the one and despise the other. You cannot serve both God and Money.

Matthew 6:24

God's Words of Life on

Stewardship

Godliness with contentment is great gain. For we brought nothing into the world, and we can take nothing out of it. But if we have food and clothing, we will be content with that. People who want to get rich fall into temptation and a trap and into many foolish and harmful desires that plunge men into ruin and destruction. For the love of money is a root of all kinds of evil. Some people, eager for money, have wandered from the faith and pierced themselves with many griefs.

1 Timothy 6:6–10

Jesus sat down opposite the place where the offerings were put and watched the crowd putting their money into the temple treasury. Many rich people threw in large amounts. But a poor widow came and put in two very small copper coins, worth only a fraction of a penny. Calling his disciples to him, Jesus said, "I tell you the truth, this poor widow has put more into the treasury than all the others. They all gave out of their wealth; but she, out of her poverty, put in everything — all she had to live on."

Mark 12:41–44

God's Words of Life on

Stewardship

"Will a man rob God? Yet you rob me. But you ask, 'How do we rob you?' In tithes and offerings. You are under a curse—the whole nation of you—because you are robbing me. Bring the whole tithe into the storehouse, that there may be food in my house. Test me in this," says the LORD Almighty, "and see if I will not throw open the floodgates of heaven and pour out so much blessing that you will not have room enough for it."

MALACHI 3:8–10

Jesus said, "Watch out! Be on your guard against all kinds of greed; a man's life does not consist in the abundance of his possessions."

LUKE 12:15

Do not worry, saying, "What shall we eat?" or "What shall we drink?" or "What shall we wear?" For the pagans run after all these things, and your heavenly Father knows that you need them. But seek first God's kingdom and his righteousness, and all these things will be given to you as well.

MATTHEW 6:31–33

God's Words of Life on

Stress

Pressure or Stress?

Stress is a complex and potentially dangerous phenomenon. If you're a leader, you may assume that stress is simply an unavoidable component of your job. Yet the apostle Paul offered advice not on stress management but on stress avoidance. Before you write off Paul as an idealistic do-gooder, remember that stress avoidance doesn't mean pressure avoidance. Paul teaches us how to turn pressure to our advantage.

Paul achieved in his lifetime more than most people dream of accomplishing. And he did so under constant harassment and powerful opposition. Paul certainly knew what pressure was all about. That's why he is so qualified to help today's leaders endure pressure without being crippled or even killed by the stress that so often accompanies it. Paul taught four principles in Philippians 3:1 —4:6:

1. Define perspective. Only when the perspective described in Philippians is adopted does Paul's "rejoice" ring true.

Stress

2. Be gentle. Someone has likened a person under the effects of stress to a car in which the driver has one foot on the accelerator and the other on the brake. Again —be gentle.

3. Trust God. Our Lord faced stressful circumstances on numerous occasions, but all of these were minor in comparison to the stress he endured from Gethsemane to the cross. He understands.

4. Live ethically. How much stress is generated by fear of being found out? Ethical people experience less stress.

Stress will inevitably creep in —and, at times, flood in. Read and heed this primer on stress avoidance.

The people in Judah said, "The strength of the laborers is giving out, and there is so much rubble that we cannot rebuild the wall." . . . . From that day on, half of my men did the work, while the other half were equipped with spears, shields, bows and armor.

Nehemiah 4:10,16

God's Words of Life on

Stress

You are awesome, O God, in your sanctuary; the God of Israel gives power and strength to his people. Praise be to God!

Psalm 68:35

Jesus said, "Come to me, all you who are weary and burdened, and I will give you rest. Take my yoke upon you and learn from me, for I am gentle and humble in heart, and you will find rest for your souls. For my yoke is easy and my burden is light."

Matthew 11:28–30

He gives strength to the weary and increases the power of the weak. Even youths grow tired and weary, and young men stumble and fall; but those who hope in the Lord will renew their strength. They will soar on wings like eagles; they will run and not grow weary, they will walk and not be faint.

Isaiah 40:29–31

Let us not become weary in doing good, for at the proper time we will reap a harvest if we do not give up.

Galatians 6:9

Stress

Remember the Sabbath day by keeping it holy. Six days you shall labor and do all your work, but the seventh day is a Sabbath to the LORD your God. On it you shall not do any work, neither you, nor your son or daughter, nor your manservant or maidservant, nor your animals, nor the alien within your gates. For in six days the LORD made the heavens and the earth, the sea, and all that is in them, but he rested on the seventh day. Therefore the LORD blessed the Sabbath day and made it holy.

Exodus 20:8–11

So do not fear, for I am with you; do not be dismayed, for I am your God. I will strengthen you and help you; I will uphold you with my righteous right hand.

Isaiah 41:10

God will refresh the weary and satisfy the faint.

Jeremiah 31:25

Be strong in the Lord and in his mighty power.

Ephesians 6:10

GOD'S WORDS OF LIFE ON

STRESS

Unless the LORD builds the house, its builders labor in vain. Unless the LORD watches over the city, the watchmen stand guard in vain. In vain you rise early and stay up late, toiling for food to eat —for he grants sleep to those he loves.

PSALM 127:1 –2

The LORD makes me lie down in green pastures, he leads me beside quiet waters, he restores my soul. He guides me in paths of righteousness for his name's sake.

PSALM 23:2 –3

Since the promise of entering God's rest still stands, let us be careful that none of you be found to have fallen short of it.

HEBREWS 4:1

By the seventh day God had finished the work he had been doing; so on the seventh day he rested from all his work.

GENESIS 2:2

Jesus said, "Come with me by yourselves to a quiet place and get some rest."

MARK 6:31

Systems & Synergy

Everyone Is Needed

According to a popular story, an orchestra had gathered to rehearse with the celebrated conductor Sir Michael Costa. As the music reached a crescendo, every instrument was being played —except for one. Distracted, the piccolo player had momentarily lost his place on the page of music. He hoped his instrument wouldn't be missed. Suddenly, Costa brought down his arm and silenced the orchestra. "Where's the piccolo?" he inquired. To a skilled conductor, and a skilled leader, every part of the system is crucial —even those that may seem less important.

Paul observed that, even though Christ's body is comprised of many members, it is still *one* body. And even though that body encompasses great diversity, every member is equally a part.

Paul's point has nothing to do with human anatomy. He wanted to ensure that every follower of Christ will feel important, will be assured that his or her contribution is crucial. No one has the right to act as though he or she is separate from the body. Nor may the members of Christ's body envy one another.

While we may wish that we were different, the bottom line is that God created each of us just as he wanted us to be and calls upon each of us to faithfully serve according to our unique calling. And as leaders, we're to view every member of our team as a crucial part of the system, helping each individual discover his or her role and play it.

The eye cannot say to the hand, "I don't need you!" And the head cannot say to the feet, "I don't need you!" On the contrary, those parts of the body that seem to be weaker are indispensable . . . . so that there should be no division in the body, but that its parts should have equal concern for each other. If one part suffers, every part suffers with it; if one part is honored, every part rejoices with it.

1 Corinthians 12:21–22,25–26

Though one may be overpowered, two can defend themselves. A cord of three strands is not quickly broken.

Ecclesiastes 4:12

God's Words of Life on

Systems & Synergy

There is one body and one Spirit —just as you were called to one hope when you were called —one Lord, one faith, one baptism; one God and Father of all, who is over all and through all and in all.

Ephesians 4:4 –6

Fear not, for I have redeemed you; I have summoned you by name; you are mine.

Isaiah 43:1

Before I formed you in the womb I knew you, before you were born I set you apart.

Jeremiah 1:5

We have different gifts, according to the grace given us. If a man's gift is prophesying, let him use it in proportion to his faith. If it is serving, let him serve; if it is teaching, let him teach; if it is encouraging, let him encourage; if it is contributing to the needs of others, let him give generously; if it is leadership, let him govern diligently; if it is showing mercy, let him do it cheerfully.

Romans 12:6 –8

God's Words of Life on

Systems & Synergy

For in him you have been enriched in every way—in all your speaking and in all your knowledge.

1 Corinthians 1:5

There are different kinds of gifts, but the same Spirit. There are different kinds of service, but the same Lord. There are different kinds of working, but the same God works all of them in all men. Now to each one the manifestation of the Spirit is given for the common good. To one there is given through the Spirit the message of wisdom, to another the message of knowledge by means of the same Spirit, to another faith by the same Spirit, to another gifts of healing by that one Spirit, to another miraculous powers, to another prophecy, to another distinguishing between spirits, to another speaking in different kinds of tongues, and to still another the interpretation of tongues. All these are the work of one and the same Spirit, and he gives them to each one, just as he determines.

1 Corinthians 12:4–11

God's Words of Life on

Systems & Synergy

If I have the gift of prophecy and can fathom all mysteries and all knowledge, and if I have a faith that can move mountains, but have not love, I am nothing.

1 Corinthians 13:2

Each one should use whatever gift he has received to serve others, faithfully administering God's grace in its various forms.

1 Peter 4:10

I wish that all men were as I am. But each man has his own gift from God; one has this gift, another has that.

1 Corinthians 7:7

God gave Solomon wisdom and very great insight, and a breadth of understanding as measureless as the sand on the seashore.

1 King 4:29

It is the spirit in a man, the breath of the Almighty, that gives him understanding.

Job 32:8

God's Words of Life on Teamwork

A Mighty Team

A mark of a great leader is how many great people will join his or her team. One who attempts mighty feats had better be capable of recruiting a mighty team. King David's team was comprised of "mighty men." Because David attempted mighty things, only the mighty could keep up with him. Those who could not keep pace could not join the team.

David did that. His was one of the most celebrated teams in the entire Old Testament. Several things stand out as we consider how David pulled his team together. First, he spent time with them in battle. These men were welded to David by the hot fires of battle. His inner circle consisted of those men who had fought alongside him. He knew their capabilities, because he had seen what they could do with his own eyes.

Second, he sacrificed for them. When three of his mighty men risked their lives to obtain drinking water for him during a battle, David refused to drink it. That act of sacrifice communicated a depth of devotion and love that had to have impressed those warriors. Third, they enjoyed victory together. Time and again David and his mighty men faced seemingly insurmountable odds and saw God deliver them.

Finally, David honored them. These men were well known throughout the land as "David's Mighty Men." That phrase served as a banner that set them apart. One thing becomes clear: David knew he couldn't do it alone. And neither can we.

The Lord God took the man and put him in the Garden of Eden to work it and take care of it.

Genesis 2:15

Six days do your work, but on the seventh day do not work, so that your ox and your donkey may rest and the slave born in your household, and the alien as well, may be refreshed.

Exodus 23:12

Lazy hands make a man poor, but diligent hands bring wealth.

Proverbs 10:4

God's Words of Life on

Teamwork

For six days, work is to be done, but the seventh day shall be your holy day, a Sabbath of rest to the LORD. Whoever does any work on it must be put to death.

Exodus 35:2

Six days you shall labor and do all your work, but the seventh day is a Sabbath to the LORD your God. On it you shall not do any work, neither you, nor your son or daughter, nor your manservant or maidservant, nor your ox, your donkey or any of your animals, nor the alien within your gates, so that your manservant and maidservant may rest, as you do.

Deuteronomy 5:13–14

He who works his land will have abundant food, but he who chases fantasies lacks judgment.

Proverbs 12:11

Whatever your hand finds to do, do it with all your might, for in the grave, where you are going, there is neither working nor planning nor knowledge nor wisdom.

Ecclesiastes 9:10

God's Words of Life on

Teamwork

Diligent hands will rule, but laziness ends in slave labor.

Proverbs 12:24

The lazy man does not roast his game, but the diligent man prizes his possessions.

Proverbs 12:27

The sluggard craves and gets nothing, but the desires of the diligent are fully satisfied.

Proverbs 13:4

Dishonest money dwindles away, but he who gathers money little by little makes it grow.

Proverbs 13:11

All hard work brings a profit, but mere talk leads only to poverty.

Proverbs 14:23

He who works his land will have abundant food, but the one who chases fantasies will have his fill of poverty.

Proverbs 28:19

God's Words of Life on

Teamwork

The laborer's appetite works for him; his hunger drives him on.

Proverbs 16:26

Do not love sleep or you will grow poor; stay awake and you will have food to spare.

Proverbs 20:13

The plans of the diligent lead to profit as surely as haste leads to poverty.

Proverbs 21:5

Do you see a man skilled in his work? He will serve before kings; he will not serve before obscure men.

Proverbs 22:29

My heart took delight in all my work, and this was the reward for all my labor.

Ecclesiastes 2:10

Sow your seed in the morning, and at evening let not your hands be idle, for you do not know which will succeed, whether this or that, or whether both will do equally well.

Ecclesiastes 11:6

God's Words of Life on

Time Management

Spending or Scheduling Time?

Moses had seen his generation wandering aimlessly in the desert. For forty years the Israelites had roamed with no specific destination in sight. In view of that seemingly futile drifting, Moses had cried out to God for some assurance of significance. Moses essentially said, "Unless we are gripped by life's brevity and place proper value on the time we have, no matter how long or short it is, we will *never* gain a wise heart."

We can employ the skills and principles of time management, buy a new calendar (even a high priced electronic one), employ a better scheduling system —all are of little benefit until we understand the value of time. Granted, we may do a better job *of scheduling* our time, but that doesn't mean we're doing a better job of *spending* that time. Knowing the difference defines wisdom!

As we grow older, we look back and wonder where the time went. Each of us is allotted a finite number of days. Are we spending those days wandering aimlessly, with no goal, no purpose in sight? Or are we numbering those days and thereby gaining a heart of wisdom?

God definitely cares about how well a person manages time. Because leaders direct others' use of time as well as their own, they double their responsibility for wise use of time. The first principle of time management is recognizing the value of time and redeeming it —buying it up and using it carefully as the priceless resource that it represents.

Teach us to number our days aright, that we may gain a heart of wisdom.

PSALM 90:12

Show me, O LORD, my life's end and the number of my days; let me know how fleeting is my life. You have made my days a mere handbreadth; the span of my years is as nothing before you. Each man's life is but a breath.. . . . Man is a mere phantom as he goes to and fro: He bustles about, but only in vain; he heaps up wealth, not knowing who will get it. But now, Lord, what do I look for? My hope is in you.

PSALM 39:4 –7

God's Words of Life on

Time Management

You do not even know what will happen tomorrow. What is your life? You are a mist that appears for a little while and then vanishes. Instead, you ought to say, "If it is the Lord's will, we will live and do this or that."

James 4:14–15

Seek the Lord while he may be found; call on him while he is near. Let the wicked forsake his way and the evil man his thoughts. Let him turn to the Lord, and he will have mercy on him, and to our God, for he will freely pardon.

Isaiah 55:6–7

Let everyone who is godly pray to you, O Lord, while you may be found; surely when the mighty waters rise, they will not reach him.

Psalm 32:6

He is our God and we are the people of his pasture, the flock under his care. Today, if you hear his voice, do not harden your hearts.

Psalm 95:7–8

God's Words of Life on

Time Management

The time is short. From now on those who have wives should live as if they had none; those who mourn, as if they did not; those who are happy, as if they were not; those who buy something, as if it were not theirs to keep; those who use the things of the world, as if not engrossed in them. For this world in its present form is passing away.

1 Corinthians 7:29–31

Jesus said, "The ground of a certain rich man produced a good crop. He thought to himself, 'What shall I do? I have no place to store my crops.' Then he said, 'This is what I'll do. I will tear down my barns and build bigger ones, and there I will store all my grain and my goods. And I'll say to myself, "You have plenty of good things laid up for many years. Take life easy; eat, drink and be merry."' But God said to him, 'You fool! This very night your life will be demanded from you. Then who will get what you have prepared for yourself?' This is how it will be with anyone who stores up things for himself but is not rich toward God."

Luke 12:16–21

God's Words of Life on

Time Management

Do this, understanding the present time. The hour has come for you to wake up from your slumber, because our salvation is nearer now than when we first believed. The night is nearly over; the day is almost here. So let us put aside the deeds of darkness and put on the armor of light.

Romans 13:11–12

Be patient, then, brothers, until the Lord's coming. See how the farmer waits for the land to yield its valuable crop and how patient he is for the autumn and spring rains. You too, be patient and stand firm, because the Lord's coming is near. Don't grumble against each other, brothers, or you will be judged. The Judge is standing at the door!

James 5:7–9

Be wise in the way you act toward outsiders; make the most of every opportunity.

Colossians 4:5

Do not boast about tomorrow, for you do not know what a day may bring forth.

Proverbs 27:1

God's Words of Life on Values

Consistent Values Yield Effective Leaders

Values are uncompromisable, undebatable truths that drive and direct behavior. They are motivational —they give us reasons why we do things; and they are restrictive — they place boundaries around behavior. Leadership literature is paying increased attention to the importance of consistent values to a leader's effectiveness.

King David said the person who enjoys the presence of God and lives a blameless life is the one who speaks the truth from his heart (Ps. 15:1 –2). Because this person values truth in his heart, his words express truth. Because he values kindness, he does his neighbor no wrong. Because he values honesty, he keeps his word. Because he values justice, he does not accept a bribe.

Leaders who are value driven reap a great benefit from the Lord. David said they would never be shaken. Regardless of what may happen around them, they can live with full confidence that the right principles have shaped their values and have guided their decisions.

That confidence will give them emotional and spiritual stability. It will enable them to be leaders whom God can use for his glory.

As you examine your own life, what values do you see as driving your behavior? Make it your goal to more completely integrate godly values into your professional and personal life.

What good is it, my brothers, if a man claims to have faith but has no deeds? Can such faith save him? Suppose a brother or sister is without clothes and daily food. If one of you says to him, "Go, I wish you well; keep warm and well fed," but does nothing about his physical needs, what good is it?

JAMES 2:14–16

In everything, do to others what you would have them do to you, for this sums up the Law and the Prophets.

MATTHEW 7:12

The entire law is summed up in a single command: "Love your neighbor as yourself."

GALATIANS 5:14

God's Words of Life on

Values

Jesus replied: "'Love the Lord your God with all your heart and with all your soul and with all your mind.' This is the first and greatest commandment. And the second is like it: 'Love your neighbor as yourself.' All the Law and the Prophets hang on these two commandments."

Matthew 22:37–40

Lord, who may dwell in your sanctuary? Who may live on your holy hill? He whose walk is blameless and who does what is righteous, who speaks the truth from his heart and has no slander on his tongue, who does his neighbor no wrong and casts no slur on his fellowman, who despises a vile man but honors those who fear the Lord, who keeps his oath even when it hurts, who lends his money without usury and does not accept a bribe against the innocent. He who does these things will never be shaken.

Psalm 15:1–5

The noble man makes noble plans, and by noble deeds he stands.

Isaiah 32:8

God's Words of Life on

Values

The fruit of the Spirit is love, joy, peace, patience, kindness, goodness, faithfulness, gentleness and self-control. Against such things there is no law.

Galatians 5:22–23

He has showed you, O man, what is good. And what does the Lord require of you? To act justly and to love mercy and to walk humbly with your God.

Micah 6:8

The things that come out of the mouth come from the heart, and these make a man "unclean." For out of the heart come evil thoughts, murder, adultery, sexual immorality, theft, false testimony, slander.

Matthew 15:18–19

Keep falsehood and lies far from me; give me neither poverty nor riches, but give me only my daily bread. Otherwise, I may have too much and disown you and say, "Who is the Lord?" Or I may become poor and steal, and so dishonor the name of my God.

Proverbs 30:8–9

God's Words of Life on

Values

Who may ascend the hill of the LORD? Who may stand in his holy place? He who has clean hands and a pure heart, who does not lift up his soul to an idol or swear by what is false.

PSALM 24:3–4

We also rejoice in our sufferings, because we know that suffering produces perseverance; perseverance, character; and character, hope.

ROMANS 5:3–4

Be careful that you do not forget the LORD your God, failing to observe his commands, his laws and his decrees that I am giving you this day.

DEUTERONOMY 8:11

If we had forgotten the name of our God or spread out our hands to a foreign god, would not God have discovered it, since he knows the secrets of the heart?

PSALM 44:20–21

Do to others as you would have them do to you.

LUKE 6:31

God's Words of Life on Vision

Godly Vision

Few things are more important to effective leadership than vision. Good leaders foresee something out there, vague as it might appear from the distance, that others don't see. Being a godly leader does play a crucial role in casting a vision for your organization too. Godly leaders who are followers of Christ must first have a vision of who God is and the future he holds for them. They must also have a sense of what God has called them to do.

The apostle Paul had both. Through a miraculous vision, he was taken into heaven where he saw images he wasn't allowed to communicate. That vision enabled him to undergo intense hardship and pain with an unwavering faith in God. But there was a second vision Paul possessed. The second was a vision of his earthly ministry. He knew God had called him to minister to the Gentiles.

It's crucial for a leader to know how to identify and cultivate a personal vision. While God may not give you a vision of heaven like Paul experienced, he will give you one of himself. Through his Word he will

Vision

show you what he is like and will give you insight into your spiritual destiny. As you seek him through his Word and through prayer, ask him to show you himself. Ask him to give you a clear image of the work he has called you to join him in accomplishing.

The eyes of the LORD range throughout the earth to strengthen those whose hearts are fully committed to him.

2 CHRONICLES 16:9

The LORD is in his holy temple; the LORD is on his heavenly throne. He observes the sons of men; his eyes examine them.

PSALM 11:4

The eyes of the LORD are on the righteous and his ears are attentive to their cry.

PSALM 34:15

Search me, O God, and know my heart; test me and know my anxious thoughts. See if there is any offensive way in me, and lead me in the way everlasting.

PSALM 139:23–24

God's Words of Life on

Vision

Do not keep talking so proudly or let your mouth speak such arrogance, for the LORD is a God who knows, and by him deeds are weighed.

1 Samuel 2:3

Faith is being sure of what we hope for and certain of what we do not see.

Hebrews 11:1

We live by faith, not by sight.

2 Corinthians 5:7

In this hope we were saved. But hope that is seen is no hope at all. Who hopes for what he already has?

Romans 8:24

We fix our eyes not on what is seen, but on what is unseen. For what is seen is temporary, but what is unseen is eternal.

2 Corinthians 4:18

He persevered because he saw him who is invisible.

Hebrews 11:27

God's Words of Life on

Vision

Blessed are the pure in heart, for they will see God.

Matthew 5:8

Elisha prayed, "O Lord, open his eyes so he may see." Then the Lord opened the servant's eyes, and he looked and saw the hills full of horses and chariots of fire all around Elisha.

2 Kings 6:17

Where there is no revelation, the people cast off restraint.

Proverbs 29:18

Jesus asked them: "Why are you talking about having no bread? Do you still not see or understand? Are your hearts hardened? Do you have eyes but fail to see, and ears but fail to hear? And don't you remember?"

Mark 8:17–18

Their eyes were opened and they recognized him, and he disappeared from their sight.

Luke 24:31

WISDOM

OUTSTANDING WISDOM

Wisdom is elusive, and it seems to be in short supply. Some people are crafty and shrewd, others are well-informed and highly educated, but few of us manifest the quiet depth of wisdom. Wisdom is the ability to use the best means at the best time to accomplish the best ends. It is not merely a matter of information or knowledge, but of skillful and practical application of the truth to the ordinary facets of life.

Here is the critical principle of wisdom: The person who refuses to act on what he or she knows, who refuses wise counsel, who ignores sage advice, will get in trouble. In the resulting despair that good information will haunt that person. All the noise will come from inside this person's own head. When he or she searches for some intelligent way out of the pit he or she has so foolishly dug, there will be no wisdom left.

The long-range view is a basic tenet of wisdom. The fool lives in the present moment while the sage considers the long-term consequences of present action. Next time you hear someone saying, "I knew better," or "Why didn't I listen?" or "How could I have been so stupid?" you will recognize this song of wisdom-after-the-fact.

Wisdom calls. Some listen. Some don't. What leader in his or her right mind would not want such a priceless tool?

God's commands make me wiser than my enemies, for they are ever with me.

PSALM 119:98

The fear of the Lord —that is wisdom, and to shun evil is understanding.

JOB 28:28

The LORD will instruct you and teach you in the way you should go; he will counsel you and watch over you.

PSALM 32:8

God said, "I guide you in the way of wisdom and lead you along straight paths. When you walk, your steps will not be hampered; when you run, you will not stumble."

PROVERBS 4:11 –12

God's Words of Life on

Wisdom

Jesus said, "Everyone who hears these words of mine and puts them into practice is like a wise man who built his house on the rock. The rain came down, the streams rose, and the winds blew and beat against that house; yet it did not fall, because it had its foundation on the rock."

Matthew 7:24–25

Get wisdom, get understanding; do not forget my words or swerve from them. Do not forsake wisdom, and she will protect you; love her, and she will watch over you. Wisdom is supreme; therefore get wisdom. Though it cost all you have, get understanding.

Proverbs 4:5–7

Where can wisdom be found? Where does understanding dwell? Man does not comprehend its worth; it cannot be found in the land of the living.

Job 28:12–13

Trust in the Lord with all your heart and lean not on your own understanding; in all your ways acknowledge him, and he will

WISDOM

make your paths straight. Do not be wise in your own eyes.

PROVERBS 3:5–7

Whether you turn to the right or to the left, your ears will hear a voice behind you, saying, "This is the way; walk in it."

ISAIAH 30:21

The wisdom that comes from heaven is first of all pure; then peace-loving, considerate, submissive, full of mercy and good fruit, impartial and sincere.

JAMES 3:17

My son, if you accept my words and store up my commands within you, turning your ear to wisdom and applying your heart to understanding, and if you call out for insight and cry aloud for understanding, and if you look for it as for silver and search for it as for hidden treasure, then you will understand the fear of the LORD and find the knowledge of God. For the LORD gives wisdom, and from his mouth come knowledge and understanding.

PROVERBS 2:1–6

Adapted from notes written by Dr. Kenneth Boa, Dr. Sid Buzzell, and Bill Perkins

Other titles to enjoy in the God's Words of Life Series include:

God's Words of Life from the Men's Devotional Bible

God's Words of Life from the Women's Devotional Bible 2

God's Words of Life from the New Student Bible

God's Words of Life from the Classics Devotional Bible